THE END

Edited By
Chris Charlesworth

Cover and book designed by
Lisa Pettibone, Four Corners Design

Picture research by
Paul Giblin & Bob Seymore

Cover Photo by
Barry Plummer

ISBN 0.7119.2398.1
Order No. OP 46093

Exclusive distributors:

Book Sales Limited
8/9 Frith Street
London W1V 5TZ, UK

Music Sales Corporation
225 Park Avenue South
New York, NY 10003, USA

Music Sales Pty Limited
120 Rothschild Avenue
Rosebery,NSW 2018, Australia

To the Music Trade only:

Music Sales Limited
8/9 Frith Street
London W1V 5TZ,UK

Typeset by
Four Corners Design

Printed in England by
St. Edmundsbury Press, Bury St. Edmunds

Every effort has been made to trace the copyright holders of the
photographs in this book but one or two were unreachable. We would be
grateful if the photographers concerned would contact us.

THE END

THE DEATH OF
JIM MORRISON

BOB SEYMORE

OMNIBUS PRESS
LONDON · NEW YORK · SYDNEY

DEDICATION:
for Hopo

Acknowledgements

THE AUTHOR is grateful to the following for their contributions to the research and production of this book: Marta de Lapresle, who started the ball rolling; Nick Gough, who was always around; Professor Austin Gresham, for free professional advice; Mr Thomas and his son Patrick, neighbours of Jim and Pam; Monsieur A. Chastagnol, Jim's neighbour in Paris and the last man outside of officials to have seen Jim's body; Richard Chainey, for the feedback; Christopher English at the US Embassy in Paris; Nadine Sim, for her dedication and patience, and her friend Marie-Laure Brilland for collecting the necessary files and paperwork; Capt. Mercier and Lt. Col. Galeraud, in Paris; Dr. Rob Stepney and Dr. Neville Silverston; Barry Miles and Chris Charlesworth for editorial advice; Danny Sugerman in Los Angeles; and finally my wife Patsy who coped in the most desperate of circumstances.

Bob Seymore, January 1991.

CHAPTER ONE

"JIM LEFT FOR Paris right in the middle of mixing 'LA Woman'. There was really no reason for Jim to be there for the mix. He said, 'You guys finish up - I'm going to Paris'. We said, 'OK man, talk to you later.' I haven't heard from him since." - *Ray Manzarek, 1981*.

"I saw Pam a few months afterwards, and when I looked into her eyes, I felt pretty much that Jim was dead... on the other hand he's just about the only person I've met who was wild enough to pull a fast one like that." - *John Densmore, 1972*.

"If Pamela was any indication, then Jim was dead. She wasn't faking it. This was a woman who was totally broken up. Jim was her total life and she was devastated, so I assume Jim was dead from her reaction and the fact that the coffin was put into the ground, and that no-one else has ever said otherwise. But... who knows?" - *Ray Manzarek, 1980*.

EVER SINCE I first heard their music, I've always loved The Doors. There was an element of menace about them that forced you to sit up and take notice; passivity was out, confrontation, participation, action was in. They were an acquired taste, never really easy on the ears, but once you'd acquired the taste The Doors and their music were wonderful.

The Doors, and singer Jim Morrison in particular, never did anything by halves. They seemed deeply committed to their music and the lifestyle that went with it, and the depth of this commitment was never likely to sit well with the guardians of law and order, the moral majority. Jim in particular found himself at odds with all and sundry during his ascendancy to rock hero status between 1967 and 1970.

From all published accounts it seems that Jim was far from blameless for the wild reputation he earned. Various biographies paint a portrait of an arrogant, selfish and generally rather unpleasant fellow. Even as a youngster there was nothing he liked better than to needle anyone and everyone who came into his orbit, and as he grew older and more threatening this included anyone in authority, absolute total strangers and even the other Doors and their entourage. It seems to be no secret that neither drummer John Densmore nor guitarist Robbie Krieger were on the best of terms with Jim for much of The Doors' career, while Ray Manzarek, who 'discovered' Jim, was only slightly more tolerant, probably because of their mutual interest and backgrounds in avant garde film making. John and Robbie were professional musicians, anxious to offer their best at every show - and reap the substantial rewards that rock stars could expect at the end of the sixties; Jim not only compromised their chances of doing this but couldn't give a damn most of the time either.

Morrison had no desire for material comforts, nor was he particularly interested in a 'career' as a musician. He often slept wherever he happened to drop. Apart from a few books - and the ubiquitous leather pants - he had few possessions, nor did he seek any form of traditional stability or security. More often than not he was drunk, stoned on grass, or both, and he seemed to take pleasure in behaving badly in public in order to embarrass the company he was with.

This last trait he sometimes tried to justify as a form of social experiment; Jim Morrison was not typical as far as rock stars go. For a start, he was exceptionally well educated in the arts, and possessed of a natural curiosity that never took things for granted. He was an avid reader of serious literature, philosophy and poetry since his early teens, an underground film buff (and student) and a man drawn towards deep philosophical arguments and anarchic experiments about human behaviour and the limits of man's endurance. Estranged from his family - especially his career naval officer father - and given to wild attention-grabbing gestures, he lurched dangerously into Southern California like a loose cannon aboard a storm-tossed warship.

Then came The Doors. He met Ray Manzarek, a classically

THE END

7

THE END

trained pianist and fellow film student, on the beach at Venice in the summer of 1965, recited some words from a poem he'd written called 'Moonlight Drive' and responded immediately to Ray's suggestion that they form a group and "make a million dollars". John Densmore and Robbie Krieger were quickly recruited - they had met Ray at a meditation class - and after some chaotic rehearsals, The Doors, named after Aldous Huxley's quote from William Blake, *The Doors Of Perception*, began playing week nights at an unfashionable club called the London Fog on Sunset Strip.

After a few false starts Elektra signed them in late 1966 and their future was assured when their stunning début album was released the following year. Twelve months on they were big stars with Jim, the leader, far and away the brightest of their galaxy.

But he was a mass of contradictions, probably schizophrenic, and the heavier the mantle of celebrity the worse his behaviour became and the more he sought to escape. The extrovert and anti-social behaviour on and off stage was the action of a man who considered himself to be a true artist who thought that people were not taking him seriously. The Doors attempted to put across something deeper than just rock and roll music but somehow they found themselves categorised amid the commercial side of the music business and not played on underground (FM) radio as much as they would have liked. Many younger fans who had not seen the group live thought of The Doors as a band who made Top 20 singles like 'Light My Fire' and 'Hello I Love You' - both number hits in the USA - and not as an album act like The Grateful Dead who never even released singles. The Doors also came from Los Angeles at a time when all the underground music, the music of The Dead and Jefferson Airplane for example, was assumed to come from San Francisco, though Frank Zappa's Mothers of Invention were from LA and the Velvet Underground was from New York and this didn't seem to stop them getting plenty of airplay on underground and college radio stations.

Being a pop star, Jim came to reason, was trivial and unsatisfying; being screamed at by teenage girls was demeaning to his talent and the nature of his art; being handsome and having his handsome face adorn posters on the bedroom walls of his fans for its handsomeness alone was insulting to his work as a writer. He wondered if he could sustain his celebrity if he allowed himself to become a fat, bearded, ugly, bloated, drunken slob. Would his fans still love him if he refused to change his clothes for a month, stopped washing and never combed his matted hair?

How far could he go in this perverse experiment? Would his fans still love him if he were no longer available, if he lived on the other side of the world, away from the madness of Southern California, or even if he was dead?

These dark thoughts were synonymous with the dark brooding music his band tried to play every night above the screams that Jim's shaman dancing and tight leather pants inspired. The Doors' music was unlike the kind of sunny fun-filled pop music that Los Angeles musicians had produced before. It was neither sunny nor fun; much of it was threatening, night-time music, in which Morrison's impressionistic lyrics and intense delivery combined with the unusually eclectic backdrop of Manzarek and Krieger to create a turbulent maelstrom of delicious but poisoned brews.

Morrison drank freely from poisoned brews during his short life. I was living in San Francisco when news of his death filtered back to America from Paris. In those days I was more interested in commercial art - making bright fluorescent posters which I tried to sell in what were called head shops. You'd walk in, there would be a smell of incense, candles were the principal source of illumination and underground music - probably Iron Butterfly playing 'In A Gadda Da Vida' - would drone out from a solitary dusty speaker. I used to make posters that glowed under ultraviolet black light, posters of Hendrix, Janis Joplin, and, yes, Jim Morrison. His long black hair curled like snakes aroused by an Arab piper, his eyes glowed from pits deep within his skull and his smile mocked authority with indecent glee.

The dream of the sixties, the Utopian hope of universal love and peace inspired in part by the music of long haired men with guitars, was shattered by the deaths of Brian Jones in 1969 and Jimi Hendrix and Janis Joplin in 1970. The final blow came the following year: Jim Morrison, leather clad lizard clown and leader of The Doors, was now dead too.

THE END

**THE
END**

The press reported that Jim had died in his Paris apartment in the early hours of the morning of July 3, 1971, from a heart-attack suffered while taking a bath. Jim Morrison the singer, Jim Morrison the poet, Jim Morrison, the voice of anti-authority, was dead. Had he crumbled under the pressure of stardom? Had he decided on that ultimate intellectual experiment to determine the truth about the enduring nature of fame? Or had he died from the delicious poisons that flowed too freely in his veins?

At first I just could not believe it. He was an enormously controversial figure who always seemed to be in some kind of trouble or another, and piling up against him in 1971 were various court cases, any one of which could end up with a jail sentence. There were paternity suits from girls of doubtful virtue, and even a trumped up charge of sky-jacking en route to Las Vegas while under the influence of alcohol, an incident which by all accounts amounted to nothing more than a member of Jim's party attempting to flirt with a stewardess by putting his hand up her skirt. More damning was the indictment for lewd and indecent behaviour likely to cause a riot during a concert at Miami in Florida in July, 1969, the famous incident where he supposedly flashed his audience and simulated masturbation on stage at the Dinner Key auditorium.

The charges were mounting up, the mood of the nation was ugly and there were many right wingers in the administration and judiciary, especially in Southern states like Florida, who thought that a spell in jail, not to mention a prison haircut, would be no bad thing for an uppity rock singer with an attitude problem like Jim Morrison. It looked as if the odds were against him, but at the same time the word was that he'd had enough of the pop scene and wanted to quit The Doors to concentrate on his writing. His first book of poetry, a compendium of two privately published works called *The Lords* and *The New Creatures*, had just gone to press in New York and Jim planned to publish more.

To get away from his legal problems and all the pressure of stardom Morrison had decided to join his long-time girlfriend Pamela Courson who was then living in Paris. Morrison arrived in France in March 1971. Only a few friends knew that

THE
END

he was there and most of the time he wasn't recognized as he strolled around the boulevards and visited book shops on the left bank in the footsteps of earlier American writers like F. Scott Fitzgerald and Ernest Hemingway. He'd shaved his famous unruly beard and taken no steps to lose the considerable weight he'd gained in the years since The Doors started. Only a relatively small number of young French people were into American rock'n'roll because of the language difficulty, so he could walk the streets and drink in cafés just like anyone else. To the French he was just another curious young American tourist.

Several months passed by and he was beginning to relax, though he continued to drink heavily and occasionally use cocaine. He was apparently trying to control his drinking but there were already signs of serious health problems; he had coughed up blood on a couple of occasions and he became out of breath easily after climbing stairs.

Then on July 3, 1971, just after midnight Jim decided to take a bath. Pamela went to bed but woke up sometime around 5:00am and realized that Jim hadn't returned to bed. She found him lying dead in the tepid water. She called for help and the first to arrive was the fire brigade resuscitation unit followed shortly afterwards by the police but it was too late. Jim was pronounced dead and on July 7, he was buried at the Père Lachaise cemetery in Paris in the company of Oscar Wilde, Edith Piaf and Molière. It was not until July 9 that the news was released to the world press by The Doors' acting manager Bill Siddons on his return to Los Angeles from Paris with Pamela.

Siddons had gone to Paris at Pam's request because she telephoned in a panic to say that something had happened to Jim. She didn't say what but Siddons obviously feared the worst and flew out at once. It wasn't the first time that rumours of Jim's death had floated but this time Siddons decided to take it seriously. When he arrived at the Morrison's apartment Pam showed him a closed coffin and a death certificate. Siddons never saw the body.

This is the reason why for years there have been rumours and speculation that Jim might still be alive, that his 'death' was all a big hoax. It seemed plausible. Jim was certainly an

THE END

impish character capable of pulling a prank such as this, and his impending legal problems suggested a likely motive. Rumour also had it that there was no record of a police investigation on file, no record of the fire brigade's attendance, and no evidence that a post-mortem examination had been conducted. The death certificate had stated that Morrison died of a heart attack but Pam couldn't remember the name of the doctor who signed the certificate. Even the American Embassy in Paris denied knowing of the death of an American citizen on that particular weekend. Before he left Los Angeles for Paris, Morrison had asked the other Doors, "What would happen to you if I died?" Was he already planning to disappear?

The press, and later his various biographers, were unable to say that Jim's death was an established fact. Did Pamela bury an empty coffin? Had Siddons, and the rest of the world, been conned by a sealed casket and a phoney death certificate? Was Jim alive and well somewhere in the world, free from the trappings of fame and the attentions of the lawmen?

Then there were other, even more fantastic, rumours: that Morrison was dead all right, but that he had died in the toilet of a late night rock club on the rue de Seine called the Rock'n'Roll Circus after taking several lines of heroin, thinking either that it was cocaine or misjudging its level of purity. The story went that he was taken out of the club across the back of the stage while a group performed a show called "The Death of Rock'n'Roll"! The Rock'n'Roll Circus communicated at its rear with the kitchens of a much more respectable club, The Alcazar, on the rue Mazarine. It was from here that he was supposedly bundled into a cab or car, dazed, in a coma or already dead, and taken home to the rue Beautreillis. It is also said that late that night, hours before the police or any of Morrison's friends were notified, Cameron Watson, the disc-jockey at La Bulle, another late night music business club, announced the death of Jim Morrison to a largely intoxicated audience. His information had supposedly come from a well known heroin addict. Was Jim Morrison another victim of drugs? Was there a cover-up? Alive or dead, the event seemed to be shrouded in mystery.

The sixties were still alive and kicking in 1971 and someone's over-stimulated imagination also caused a rumour to spread that Jim was still alive but had been abducted by aliens from outer space. This idea I dismissed (14 years later), but there was something enormously romantic in the idea that Morrison was alive and well and living somewhere in the African bush, dancing naked by moonlight in the company of native tribesmen and the odd witch doctor or two.

Of course, the mystery of Jim's death was a major factor in the continuing popularity of The Doors and the fascination that has attached itself to Morrison down the years. So long as people believed in the myth that he might be alive, then there was a talking point which created and perpetuated interest in the band and Morrison in particular. This is good for business, as those with a continuing financial interest in Morrison's legacy have surely appreciated over the years.

Jim Morrison has become a cult figure, romanticised alongside icons like James Dean and Marilyn Monroe. Long after his death Doors' albums continue to sell in their hundreds of thousands. Many an intact band still performing would happily swop their annual royalty cheque for those that Elektra's business affairs department make over to the three surviving Doors come accounting time. Their music continues to inspire young bands, their songs are covered time and again and their sense of disaffected style is emulated down the years by angry young men with guitars, drums and black leather jackets.

Much of this would undoubtedly have occurred had Jim Morrison not died in his bath that night in Paris, but like only a handful of sixties icons, The Doors not only refuse to die but continue to exert an omnipresent influence on music and ideas in the 90s.

And in the meantime the legend of Jim Morrison has grown bigger and bigger, like the giant redwood trees in the state where he chose to live.

THE END

CHAPTER TWO

THE END Onε εvεning I was in Sweeney Todd's Pizza Parlour in Cambridge with my friend Richard when we got to talking about Jim Morrison and The Doors. Richard and I talked a lot about music and the good old days when we had a band together. The band was called Hopo and very nearly got signed up by Private Stock who did Blondie's first album, but it all fell through like so many deals with so many bands and so many record companies. They were supposed to see us at a gig but we don't even know if they came or not. Then in 1980 various members of the band went off in separate directions.

I became self-employed and began operating a photographic business. We've been going now for ten years. We're doing reasonably well, specializing in press photography, studio and location work, local advertising work.

So I told my friend Richard that I thought there was a strong possibility that Jim Morrison was alive and well because of all the mystery and uncertainty surrounding his death. Richard agreed that it was probable but unlikely. Then I started seeing these posters of Morrison everywhere; a Doors revival. One evening I watched *Apocalypse Now*, on television. I never got a chance to see it in the movies. Then all of a sudden, the opening bars of 'The End' came on, and I thought, "I'd better do something about this." I sat and listened to the song and decided to look into it methodically. It was as though I was in the middle of a reunion with an old and forgotten friend, and once reunited the memories of a fond but distant past came flooding back.

As far as I could tell, Morrison's death had never been investigated properly. All the reports were just rumours. Was he alive or was he dead? I had the feeling that maybe he was alive because of the rumours and I thought what it would be worth to get a photograph of him, somewhere. That's what I wanted to do, to get that picture of Jim Morrison nearly 20 years on. That was my ambition. I was still relatively young and new on the scene of photo-journalism but I told Richard that I was going to start my research and if Jim Morrison was alive I was the man who was going to find him and photograph him. It would be the scoop of the decade.

My office is tiny; a desk covered in paper, rubbish and everything, with no room to work, just enough space to put my diary and answer the phone. I have a picture transmitter so we can transmit photographs to any newspaper in the world within eight minutes, so we try to be a press agency when there's work going on in the area, but it's not that frequent. So several months went by and I spent most of my time taking photographs or locked in the darkroom developing them. I had previously employed a French girl, Marta, but she eventually moved back to Paris. This gave me an opportunity to make some preliminary enquiries there. I asked her to contact the American Embassy, find any press cuttings that reported the death, try to get a copy of the death certificate or any police records, find out who handled the funeral and search for any inconsistencies that might turn up. All basic starting points of an investigation.

Marta was very nice. She was a foreign student who settled in Cambridge, she was a very excitable sort of person, with great aspirations to be an artistic photographer. I was giving her training in printing and dark room techniques, but she also expressed an interest in the Morrison project though she believed personally that Morrison was dead, so she did a lot of work off her own bat. Then she had difficulties with her job and found out how hard it was to transcend all the red tape if you didn't have proper authorisation.

It turned out that press cuttings were scarce but anything she might obtain would provide trails to explore. I didn't realize then that these basic enquiries would lead to numerous further questions, some of them unanswerable, and that if there had been a cover-up, it had been very well done. The only thing Marta was able to come up with was an extract from Jim Morrison's death certificate which she got from the Office of Births and Deaths. They will give you an extract from the

THE END

15

death certificate but you can't see the original without special permission because it is confidential, and permission is rarely granted. The extract just states who reported the death and what time and date the death occurred. It does not provide the name of the doctor who signed the certificate. It read as follows:

> *The third of July nineteen seventy-one, five o'clock, died, 17 rue Beautreillis, JAMES DOUGLAS MORRISON, born Florida (United States of America) 8 December, 1943, writer, home in Los Angeles (U.S.A.) 82-16 Norton Ave., Los Angeles, next of kin not known to the informant. Bachelor. Reported 3 July, 1971, 2:30pm by declaration of MICHEL GAGNEPAIN, 34 years old, employed 8 rue du Cloître-Nôtre-Dame, who after reading the declaration has signed in our presence. Annie Jacqueline Françoise TARIN, the wife of MORENO, civil servant of the Paris 4th arrondissement. Civil Status Officer by the delegated authority of the Mayor. AM.*

Marta gave up. My commitments in Cambridge made it too difficult for me to go to Paris right then so I shelved the project for a while. But I didn't forget about it.

It was in July 1988 that I decided to start up again and do what I could from this end, so on July 21, I telexed the American Embassy in Paris, asking them if they had any records concerning the death of James Douglas Morrison, and if so, could they tell me the following :

When, how and who reported Mr. Morrison's death to them?

The official cause of death and from what source they received this information?

What was the Embassy's involvement in informing next of kin in the U.S.A.?

What did they know about the disposal of Mr. Morrison's personal belongings?

Who now had legal jurisdiction over Mr. Morrison's remains?

Did they have any documented evidence on Mr. Morrison's travels in Europe just prior to his death?

And finally, did they know which next of kin attended Mr. Morrison's funeral?

I played up the fact that I was an American citizen and that I was a freelance journalist, hoping that they would say, "There's one of our boys here, let's give him some help." No way. On July 26 the reply came:

THE
END

Dear Mr. Seymore,

We are in receipt of your July telex requesting details about the 1971 decease of Jim Morrison in Paris.
For information concerning this case, I refer you to the deceased's family's legal representatives in the U.S.: Weinstock, Manion, King, Hardie, & Reisman, 1888 Century Park East, Suite 800, Los Angeles, CA 90067, U.S.A. (0101-213-553-8844).
They will determine how much information concerning this case may be made available to you.
I hope you find the above information helpful.

Sincerely,
Christopher English,
American Consul.

Well, the last thing I wanted to do was to contact the Morrison family lawyers simply because if Jim were alive it was always possible that they were involved in the conspiracy; arranging his finances and so on. If I approached them, they would tip him off and he would go to ground. I shelved the project again until I could find a better way to approach the research.

It was more than a year later, in October 1989, when I re-opened the case. I had just read *No One Here Gets Out Alive* by Jerry Hopkins and Danny Sugerman which gave me a new drive to investigate the death of Jim Morrison and complete it once and for all. Aside from being a compelling and very readable, if controversial, account of the life of Jim Morrison, this book stressed the possibility of Jim being alive still. Its publication - and subsequent best seller status - went a long way towards re-establishing the popularity of The Doors

17

THE END

among young Americans in the early eighties.

At that time my wife and I took in students from a local Cambridge language school, so I asked the school to assist me with letters that had to be written in French. They introduced me to Nadine Sim who became my interpreter and an invaluable assistant. Nadine is French, in her thirties. She's got short dark hair, medium build, not fat, not thin, and she speaks perfect English. She's married to a Scot and though she's lived in England for some time she often goes back to France. She spent several years in Scotland when she was a student in Edinburgh and this accounts for her pleasantly unusual accent: a soft French-Scottish brogue which is very easy on the ears.

There was a number of obvious avenues to explore. I asked Nadine to phone the Père Lachaise cemetery to get all the data on the grave. They told her she would have to put her request in writing, so I wrote a letter which she translated.

Dear Sir,

I am an American freelance photojournalist living and working in England. I am currently doing research on a James Douglas Morrison who is buried in your cemetery. He died July 3, 1971.

It is not possible for me to come and ask these questions in person, therefore I would be grateful if you could answer them:-

1) On what date was the grave plot purchased?

2) How was it paid for, cheque or cash?

3) Who paid for it and who selected its position?

4) On what date was the funeral?

5) Who performed the service?

6) How did the coffin arrive at the cemetery and which funeral directors, if any, brought it?

I would appreciate any help you can give me or suggest anyone who can.

Yours sincerely,
BOB SEYMORE.

THE END

About a month passed by and I was still waiting for a reply. In the end I asked Nadine to telephone Père Lachaise to see if they had any intention of replying. Some lady in their office there said that they had written a reply and that it had been posted to me. I should receive it any day. Okay, I waited for the letter. Days went by. No letter was to be seen. Nadine phoned again and this time they admitted that no reply had been written.

What in hell was going on? I'd always thought French bureaucrats were supposed to be efficient. Their excuse for such blatant deceit was that the information I required was of a "confidential" nature and they were not permitted to answer such questions. So why did they ask me to write in the first place? Nadine told them what she thought of them and eventually they gave in and said they could answer two of my questions. The grave was purchased on July 2, 1971 and the burial was on July 7, 1971. That was all they could tell me. The conversation ended.

I was staggered. This was amazing! Jim Morrison bought himself a grave *the day before he died!* Already my research was paying off. It was beginning to look good. Too good, actually. It couldn't be this easy to uncover a hoax. I realized that I was getting too excited. After all, this might just be an administrative mistake. It was important to get the information in writing. Nadine phoned Paris again but this time they gave her a different answer: the grave was bought on July 7, 1971 and the burial also took place on the seventh.

The call was completed and I deliberated on this new information. It was clear that I was dealing with complete idiots and this first hurdle was already giving me problems. It didn't make sense at all. How can anyone buy a grave and be buried on the same day? A feeling of gloom descended. I could tell that I was in for a long haul. This was getting bloody ridiculous. Nadine phoned once more to ask how this could be

19

THE END

and the cemetery official agreed that it was not possible. This time they actually bothered to look up the information in the files. There they discovered that the grave was purchased on July 6 and the burial took place the following day. This made sense. They agreed to mail a photo-copy of the register entry as confirmation.

Although it was useful to have the accurate facts, it was still something of a let down because for a moment I thought we had discovered something very suspicious. Had Jim himself bought the grave on the day before he 'died', then it would have been clear that he either intended to die the following day or, more likely, intended to pretend to die. In the event it was obviously a clerical error. The burial was legitimate as the documents showed when they eventually arrived. The register did show one curious thing: it was a double grave but Jim was the only person interred within it. Pamela Courson died in 1974 and was buried in the States. Why the extra space? Had she intended to join him when she died? Instead of getting answers, more questions were inconveniently popping up. This wasn't what I wanted. Could this be a good sign? It certainly wasn't going to be a straightforward investigation but it was early days yet.

So far, I was able to confirm that something or someone was buried in Jim Morrison's grave at Père Lachaise. I remembered what my friend Richard had said, "Only you Bob could go off and prove someone was already dead." I felt a slight twinge of doubt and hoped I wasn't going to make myself look foolish. I knew I could only get to the bottom of this in Paris, so the next move was obviously to go there. Since my French is virtually non existent, I took Nadine with me as my translator. I was now committed to the investigation. I mean, I was spending my own money on a "spec" story. I had to get something out of it.

We left on January 14, taking the Hovercraft car ferry from Dover to Calais, a Doors cassette playing as we drove south east towards the French capital. Nadine had booked us into the Grand Hotel Malher, a one star hotel on rue Malher in the 4th arrondissement, a few blocks from Jim's old apartment. It took an hour to find a parking space and check in, and though it was already dark, I couldn't resist walking over to the rue Beautreillis and seeing the building where Pam and Jim had stayed. There it was, this was where he lived, this was where he died. It was a dark January evening but I could just see this gloomy building towering up before me like a monument to its famous former occupant. If only the walls could speak.

THE END

I stood there for a while, wondering how different the building looked in 1971 when Jim and Pam lived there, which way Jim would turn when he came out on to the street, which way he would walk, which road, which directions he would go in. The restaurant opposite... would he have eaten there? Nadine and I just walked around. It was too late to start asking questions.

It was somewhat depressing to see where Jim had met his Maker and to think that so many years had passed by so quickly. I remember those times so clearly as though it were yesterday. Time is so unkind. I felt as though I had come too late and that the trail was already cold. It was hard to believe that this was the place he was found dead. That night, after a good dinner, I had a nagging feeling that Jim was actually dead after all and my efforts were in vain. What was I doing there? Was this going to prove a pointless exercise? Was my common sense blinded by my fantasies of being a great journalist and getting the scoop of a lifetime? But it was only the first day and I hadn't even given it a chance yet. I composed myself. There are too many questions for me to let Jim Morrison rest in peace just yet. I had to see it through. I missed my wife Patsy, and my children Sarah and Rebekah. I had a rough night.

The bed felt like a hammock and the noise from outside was deafening. Cars roared up the narrow street, people yelled and laughed and the street lamps shone in through my window, illuminating the room. Eventually I managed to drift off to sleep but I awoke around 5am to the flashing of a yellow hazard light and the sound of a large truck revving its engine. By now garbage cans were flying around, crashing and banging against the pavement, and the garbage men joined in the chorus, yelling at each other coarsely in their native language. As they made their way up the street the noise subsided and eventually blended in with the rest of the Paris dawn chorus,

THE END

and I drifted off once more, dozing fitfully.

After breakfast our first port of call was the local Police Station for the 4th arrondissement on the rue de Rivoli. There we were told to go to the Town Hall just across the road. It was early on a Monday morning and the receptionist was still shaking off the weekend's malaise when we arrived. She was certainly not overjoyed to be confronted by us with our unusual requests first thing on a Monday morning. She said that the police records, if any, were kept at Police HQ on the Ile de la Cité.

Since we were actually in the Town Hall, it seemed sensible to try and get a copy of the death certificate. The head of the department of registration of births and deaths met us and told us that they had the records but she could not show them to me as they were confidential. She had the cold emotionless expression of someone who hates her job but as long as she was doing it, she was going to make the most out of what little power she had. I asked what was the cause of death?

"I know what he died of, but I can't tell you," she replied. She didn't smile. Nor did I. I got the distinct feeling she was teasing me. She was holding the information I needed right there in front of me, just beyond my reach... and there wasn't a damn thing I could do about it.

After lunch it was time to check out the Fire Brigade. Morrison's apartment was in the 4th arrondissement, the responsibility of the 11th Regiment on the rue de Sevigne. We arrived at the front gate reception saying we had some inquiries that we would like to make, expecting to get the usual run-around. But no. To our surprise they said, "Oh yes yes, come through. Captain Mercier's expecting you."

How could this be? But they said, "Yeah, yeah, come through," so we went.

Through a courtyard, into this nice office, stone floor, sturdy desk, photographs on the walls of fire brigade regalia, flags, it was a comfortable room. Captain Mercier was sitting there, and he stood up, shook hands, and said, "I've been expecting you," but when we told him who we were, he said, "Oh, I thought you were someone else." End of mystery.

We explained to him what we wanted to do and he agreed to continue the interview and see if he could be of assistance.

French Fire Brigade personnel are incredibly fit men, trained like an army on manoeuvres, and they have the same sort of respect for each other as professional soldiers have for their fellows in arms. He was quite tall and wore a blue jacket, black army boots, and blue trousers tucked in to the top. He was in his late twenties or early thirties, he sat bolt upright in his chair, and carried himself with the bearing of a very composed military man. He was clean shaven with short dark hair.

Captain Mercier said all the information we needed was confidential. I was expecting this, and agreed saying, "Obviously you can't tell us the details of the case, but surely you can confirm whether or not you were there." I explained that all I was trying to establish was whether or not an incident did take place at the time and whether or not the fire brigade was called out to this incident. This would at least enable me to confirm that an incident did take place and surely this information would not be confidential, especially after so long.

But the information wasn't there anyway. It was kept at headquarters, over on the other side of town, but he said he doubted if they would give us any information. "Who is this American that you are looking for?" he asked at this point. "Why are you here?"

So I crossed my fingers and told the Captain that I had just flown in from the States, all this way, for this biography I was writing, and I needed their help. I couldn't go back with nothing. I had no intention of writing a book then, it just seemed a good cover.

"Who is this person?" he asked again.

"Jim Morrison… Jim Morrison of The Doors," I replied.

His eyes lit up. "What? The Doors?"

He said he didn't know Morrison had died here in Paris, let alone that he was buried here. Then he began mentioning song titles… 'The End' and 'L.A. Woman'.

"Yeah, that's right," I said, looking straight into his eyes and nodding as though we were on common ground with a language of our own. We had an understanding.

He picked up his telephone and dialled headquarters to make enquiries with the archives department.

"Got two people here who want some information," he said into the receiver. "Find the particular case. Obviously they can't be given the details but can you help them out just to show them whether or not we were involved." He organized an appointment for us and told us they were expecting our visit.

The Fire Brigade Headquarters was a large building over in the 17th arrondissement. It's odd shaped with a huge internal courtyard with cars parked, a guard at the entrance with a barrier that lifts up to admit vehicles. On the day we went some unfortunate fellow was perched up on the top of his fire engine ladder cleaning the windows in full kit.

We had to identify ourselves, then we were directed to the archives department and given a form to fill in, outlining the information we required. An officer soon came and introduced himself and asked us what exactly we wanted to know.

I told him that it was important for us to know whether or not the brigade answered the emergency call concerning the events of July 3, 1971. He immediately said he could not give this information as it was confidential. By now I was beginning to get very tired of hearing that word but we pressed on anyway. Through Nadine I explained that it was not the details of their report I was interested in. I just wanted confirmation that they were actually involved in the case, that they had a file on it and could they confirm it in writing please.

"Why do you want to know this?" he asked.

Out came the old story, that I was researching for a biography that I was writing and so on. It was better than telling them I was just a freelance journalist. I have discovered from experience that a freelance journalist is often turned away whenever they come knocking on doors simply because they do not represent a publication and therefore have no credibility. I was determined not to allow this to happen.

"No problem," he said. "Come back tomorrow before lunch and we will give you a letter as requested."

Finally we were getting somewhere and could establish if there was an incident or not. If the fire brigade turned out not to have been involved, we would have uncovered something very suspicious indeed. We thanked him and said we would see them tomorrow.

Earlier in the day we visited the law court where the police archives are kept and requested a meeting with the press officer, but this was not possible. The press office asked us to state in writing what exactly we wanted. Nadine drafted a letter in French and handed it in. We were told an answer would follow in due course. They would contact us at our hotel. I hoped. Nothing but red-tape on this case.

After our visit to Fire Brigade H.Q. we took the Metro back across Paris to the apartment where Jim and Pam had lived during their stay in Paris. The rue Beautreillis is a quiet back street in the Marais, a beautiful area of sizeable seventeenth century town houses known as Hôtels which in Morrison's day were mostly still being restored. Located in the 4th arrondissement, in the centre of the city, it is close to the old Jewish neighbourhood, and also the oldest square in Paris, the Place Des Vosges. It is one of the oldest and most attractive parts of Paris. I could understand why they'd settled there.

There is a restaurant across the street from number 17 but I couldn't tell whether or not it was there when Jim lived opposite. Jim's building is very tall for Paris, with double green doors which lead through the building to another pair of doors and an internal courtyard. It was immaculately clean and well maintained. This was certainly not a cheap building, not that I had expected Jim and Pamela to be living anywhere other than in a luxury block since prior to this they had stayed at L'Hôtel on the rue des Beaux Arts, a fashionable and exclusive hotel catering to the artistic jet set.

Thanks to the success The Doors had achieved, Jim was not short of cash.

To the left and right of the doors were the intercom systems for the staircases, pigeonhole mailboxes and the concierge. We tried to interview the people living in Jim's old apartment but they said they were fed up with people coming round.

"We've had over 300 journalists come here in the six years we've lived here and we're absolutely fed up with it and we don't want to know so just go away," they told us in no uncertain terms. Or words to that effect.

We told them that we had come across some information that would put this whole thing to rest and that they wouldn't be bothered ever again, but the woman simply said, "What makes you think you're any different?"

"We'd like to speak to you," I persisted. "We'd like all the information we can get because it all helps."

THE
END

25

THE END

"No, not interested," she replied, adding that she had even had the film company come round, Oliver Stone's company doing location research and had told them the same thing: they weren't interested. I couldn't really blame them, but I had to try. I found out from the concierge that the film company asked him for a plan of the apartment so they could recreate it on their set.

We walked around the internal courtyard and I took a few pictures. Then we noticed a gentleman in his sixties looking through his mail box. It was obvious he was a resident so we introduced ourselves to him and explained why we were there. He was glad to help and said he had lived there since the days of Morrison but his memory of those times was somewhat vague.

His name was Mr Thomas. He was in his sixties with greyish hair, thin on top. He seemed a very kind man, quite friendly, retired. As Mr. Thomas was talking, one of his neighbours walked by, held out his hand to be shaken by our new friend and introduced himself as Jim Morrison, smiled and went on by. We all laughed and found it very amusing, even if it was a joke at our expense. Hopefully, all the other residents were going to be as amenable.

He recalled that Morrison was the one who died in the bath.

What else could he remember?

He said that Jim and his girlfriend used to light their rooms with candles. Mr. Thomas's apartment was a floor higher than the Morrison apartment and overlooked it from the other side of the internal courtyard.

Could he remember anything about Morrison's drinking habits?

No. He didn't recall anything like that. I thought perhaps he might have seen Jim returning to his apartment after one of his drinking bouts but Mr. Thomas thought Mr. Morrison had been very discreet about his personal habits.

We thanked Mr. Thomas for his help and asked if it would be all right to telephone him should we need any further help? He'd be glad to hear from us. Nadine and I walked back to our Hotel where we were told that the police had telephoned but it was now too late to return their call. We would have to phone them the following morning.

Nadine and I returned to the hotel after dinner and retired to our respective rooms. I wished the bed was more inviting, that the street lights weren't so bright and that the garbage men weren't so noisy but it was a re-run of the previous night, with the added attraction of an equally noisy water-hosing truck designed to wash away the piles of dog-crap that is everywhere on the streets and pavements of Paris. Inevitably it turned out to be another restless night.

The next morning, after another delicious breakfast, we returned the call to the police. As usual they wanted to know my reasons for investigating Jim Morrison's death. We told them all about the biography I was supposedly writing. We told the woman that we wanted to know if there was any police intervention in this case. She said she would phone back later.

Next on our schedule was Père Lachaise, the cemetery where Jim Morrison is buried. I wanted to ask the officials there a few questions.

Monsieur Braux at Père Lachaise was middle aged, casually dressed, with short dark mousy hair and a deep voice. He was not there when Morrison was buried but had clearly been at Père Lachaise a long time. He was pleasant enough as office people go and was expecting us and had his notes already written out.

Naturally he said that he couldn't answer any questions until he had authorization and handed us a form to fill in to be faxed to his Head Office. He said it would take at least a half hour to receive a reply so we went to visit Morrison's grave. I offered to give him my questions in advance but he didn't want to know. He gave me a map of the cemetery and marked the location of Jim's grave. "You can't miss it," he said. "The area is covered in graffiti."

It certainly is. Over the years Doors fans have succeeded in making the whole area look like a back alley off the Bowery. Morrison's grave is so defaced with graffiti that his name is barely legible. The first impression is that the grave is small in relation to the others that surround it, that Jim's final resting place could actually be a pauper's grave. Elsewhere in the cemetery the graves look like monuments to the gods but Jim's grave is sad and pathetic, and certainly not in keeping with the stature of its occupant. The headstone was at an angle where

THE END

27

THE END

someone had attempted to steal it and every corner has been chipped away by souvenir hunting fans. All the surrounding mausoleums have also been defaced and the route to the grave has been crudely signposted by fans who've scrawled "Jim" with an arrow pointing in the right direction.

It is a squalid monument to the Lizard King that ought to have been maintained properly by his family and heirs. Only a tiny percentage of the money that Jim has earned for others since his death would be required to maintain a modicum of dignity for the grave site.

Other more respectful fans have left flowers. One small bunch was sticking out of a beer can; other fans had left empty whiskey bottles and other tokens of their esteem. Years before a bust of Jim had graced the headstone but it was stolen and now probably sits on a fan's mantlepiece. From the photographs I've seen it was a good likeness. All the time we were there I couldn't stop hoping that the grave was empty and that all of this was a hoax, but if he were truly buried there then it was a sad and pathetic tribute to such a talent.

Back at the office, French bureaucracy was as efficient as ever, and no fax had been received from Head Office. I got the feeling Monsieur Braux felt a little awkward because he asked for the questions I had wanted to give him in the first place. He was able to answer most of them. Pamela had bought a double plot simply because that was all they had available at such short notice. He told us that the coffin was five metres down, covered in earth with space for another coffin and for cremated relatives should there ever be any. As far as Père Lachaise went, this was an economy model since most of the surrounding graves were family mausoleums where coffins were placed on stone shelves.

While Monsieur Braux was faxing our questions, Nadine cast an eye over the counter at his notes and spotted something. "Pamela's put down cousin," she told me.

This was odd. Why would she describe herself as that? Even more intriguing was an amendment made by Pamela's lawyers in 1977, three years after her death, changing the relationship from "cousin" to "wife". The estate was settled just before she died. Well, it was obvious that we'd seen the notes so we came right out and asked the French official if we could have a

THE
END

photocopy of them.

"Yeah," he said. "That's no problem."

So I asked him to stamp it as well, to authenticate it, and he did. I asked him why she put "cousin," but he didn't know. I didn't think he would. They really weren't interested but they liked the novelty that Morrison was buried in their cemetery.

Their files confirmed that the purchase of the plot was made on July 6, 1971, and that the funeral took place the following day. I wanted to know whether or not the purchase was made by cash or cheque, but just as the last words left my lips and Nadine was about to translate, a very important Monsieur Jean-Jacques Le Forestier walked up behind Monsieur Braux with the reply to our fax in his hand.

"None of your business," he said in an authoritative manner.

I was, of course, already quite experienced in dealing with such situations and told him I was not in the least bit interested in how much she paid to acquire the grave, just in whether or not she was the one to make the transaction. I thought that maybe Jim had signed the cheque, which would of course have been proof of his continued existence.

"Of course she was. It's not possible for anyone else to make such an arrangement," he told us with a pompous air of superiority.

I suggested that it might have been paid for on Morrison's account. But Monsieur Forestier was adamant. "Because when someone dies the banks close the accounts, that is why," he said.

I explained that Morrison's death remained a secret for nearly a week so it was quite possible the banks did not know but he did not want to continue this discussion. He said they were authorized to answer administrative questions only. Okay, so I repeated my original question, could anyone other than Pamela have paid for the grave?

Again he said no, but then turned to his staff and asked one of the young women what she thought. Hesitantly, she volunteered the opinion that it was possible for someone else to have made the transaction. Exit Monsieur Jean-Jacques Le Forestier mumbling under his breath and shaking his head. Monsieur Braux said he would get the necessary paperwork and send me photo-copies the following week but he still

needed a letter from us requesting the information. This we
did on the spot and handed in before we left.

I was puzzled by Pamela's use of "cousin" on the request
form and by the fact that the lawyers had changed it all those
years after her death. Her lawyers must have gone through
everything that she ever signed in France. What were they
looking for? Who were they trying to protect? She was getting
at least a quarter of the royalties on the sales of The Doors
records, not to mention Jim's share of the publishing royalties,
which was a fantastic amount of money.

Our next appointment was at the Fire Brigade H.Q. as
arranged. The officer in the reception recognised us and
allowed us to pass. Pretty soon we were talking to Lieutenant
Colonel Galeraud. As far as I could make out, he was the top
brass there. He was of medium height and build, and bald
except for a little dark hair round the sides. He seemed to be
sympathetic and could understand English but he couldn't
speak it, so when I was talking he would answer the question
before Nadine had time to translate it. He was very intelligent,
very sharp and on the ball. He would listen very carefully to
what we had to say, very polite, very cordial, if he could help
he would, but he would only do what he could do to the letter.

He handed me a letter of confirmation: "I am honoured to
report that the Fire Brigade was involved and did attend the
scene on July 3, 1971," he said. He also confirmed that the fire
crew found a body in the bath with the person's head above
the water at the address that Jim and Pam were living.

Now this was not what I wanted to hear. The mystery was
beginning to crumble away. Were my eyes and ears deceiving
me? Was this the end? My spirits dropped as I half smiled out
of politeness and in appreciation for his trouble while looking
down at the letter just handed to me. He continued to tell me
that Pam was there at the scene and was assisted by a
neighbour who helped translate to the firecrew. Lieutenant
Colonel Galeraud said he was only giving this information as a
favour but was not permitted to say any more.

We then showed him an extract from the book *No One Here
Gets Out Alive* which is generally regarded as the "official"
explanation concerning the events of that fateful morning back
in 1971. In a nutshell, it gives the following explanation:

Pam and Jim were alone at the flat (sometime after midnight, Saturday, July 3, 1971) when Jim regurgitated a small quantity of blood. He had done this before, Pam said, and although she was concerned, she was not really upset. Jim claimed he felt okay and said he going to take a bath. Pamela fell asleep again. At five she woke, saw Jim had not returned to bed, went into the bathroom, and found him in the tub, his arms resting on the porcelain sides, his head back, his long, wet hair matted against the rim, a boyish smile across his clean-shaven face. At first Pamela thought he was playing one of his macabre jokes, but then she called the fire department's resuscitation unit. A doctor and the police followed, Pamela said, but all were too late.

After Nadine translated this passage for Lieutenant Colonel Galeraud he immediately consulted one of his officers and then began to get what I would usually describe as paranoid. A worried look crossed his face.

"What are your intentions with this letter?" he asked. He was concerned that I might use his letter to dispute the book. I reassured him that the book was only being used for reference. He wanted an assurance from me that I would not publish his letter to which I willingly agreed. I'd say anything just to get his letter and get out of there. I asked him whether the book matched their records of the incident? He held the file in his hands and eventually said, "Yes." I looked longingly at that file. I'm sure it would have made fantastic reading.

Nadine and I left the building and went to find a phone booth to make a few calls to England. Along the way I was stamping and swearing. Nadine must have thought I was behaving like a spoilt child. I was feeling really low, willing to call it quits and head for home. There didn't seem to be much point in carrying on. I had managed to prove that the fire department were involved and at last there was a real corpse. It now seemed that Jim Morrison's death was an established fact. The body just had to be Jim's. It was ridiculous to believe it could still be a hoax unless Morrison went to exceptional lengths to obtain a body, not an easy thing to do, particularly in a foreign country where you don't speak the language. I was clutching at straws, the desperate actions of someone who refuses to believe that his idol was dead. But I wasn't that obsessed. No way could the

THE
END

31

**THE
END**

fire department's report be fiction. It was all too real. That was the trouble. I don't know how Nadine felt about this. Perhaps she was sympathetic, but she was just doing her job. I felt very alone.

Lieutenant Colonel Galeraud had pointed out that the details of the circumstances surrounding Jim's death were all based on Pamela's testimony. There was no other verification. She could have said what she liked. He also suggested that we enquire at the Medical Institute to see if Morrison's body went there for a post-mortem examination. These were lines of enquiry worth following up.

I placed the key in the door of my hotel room, dropped my heavy camera bag and fell backwards on to the sagging bed. Lying staring at the ceiling, mustering up whatever strength I had in reserve, I cleared my head and psyched myself up for more phone calls. After 45 minutes Nadine came through to my room and yet again we started on a round of calls, starting with the Police HQ who answered but were unable to connect us with the correct department. Patience, patience, patience.

Nadine called the records office of the Medical Institute and gave them Jim Morrison's particulars: date of birth, date of death, nationality, and place of residence in Paris. The woman said she would check their files and suggested we phone again the following morning. Mr. Thomas, Morrison's former neighbour, was also on our list to phone just in case we had jogged his memory and he had remembered something of use. He was pleased to hear from us. He thought his son Patrick would remember a lot more and said he would phone us back after he had spoken to him. Helpful as ever, Mr. Thomas called back a while later and gave us his son's telephone number. We phoned Patrick straight away.

In 1971 Patrick was 12 years old but he hadn't known Jim was actually living in his apartment block at the time, even though he had a large poster of The Doors on his bedroom wall. He remembered the rumours and the events of Jim's death. There was, he recalled, one neighbour who had called the police because there was a bad smell in the building's public areas, and the source of the nuisance was Morrison's apartment. The police forced entry and discovered Jim Morrison dead in the bathroom. The floor was littered with candles and bottles of alcohol. He had been dead for several days and it was hot July weather.

He said he would contact other residents there to verify the story and would write and tell me what he discovered. Nadine thanked him and put the phone down. The room fell silent. I stared at Nadine and she back at me. This was awful. How bizarre! This was incredibly sad and pathetic. If this were true, then Morrison died alone. Pamela had done a disappearing act, returning to find him dead.

But this didn't make sense as a story, because the dates didn't fit with the official account. Morrison was last seen alive on July 2 and his death was filed on July 3. The fire brigade report confirmed the date of death as July 3. So what was going on? I knew Morrison's coffin had probably been placed in the apartment on July 6 because that's when Bill Siddons, The Doors' acting manager arrived from Los Angeles, and the funeral was on the following day. Something was wrong here, but what? I was more confused than ever. The implications of this story suggested a drug overdose, accidental death, murder, or death by misadventure. Could this be the reason why Pamela lied about her relationship to Jim at Père Lachaise? That made sense. Maybe she didn't want anyone to know she was away at the time of Jim's death when it was known that he was unwell. The story was no longer as simple as I thought.

The next morning Nadine and I went down as usual for breakfast but this time we were met by the proprietor's geriatric dog, a beast suffering from mange, bad breath and a plethora of other canine ailments, and guaranteed, with its cathartic eyes, to put all the guests off their breakfast.

After we'd eaten Nadine telephoned the Medical Institute. They confirmed that Jim Morrison's body did not go to them for a post-mortem examination. The woman said she had checked on their computer. Another call confirmed that the police did attend the scene on that date and that the relevant file was in the Law Court archives. A Classical Enquiry was held to look into the case. More information could be obtained via the Law Court but they would expect the request in writing - naturally.

Now we had proof that the police were involved. A police

THE
END

THE END

record had been made, and they even held an enquiry into the matter. Brilliant. We were getting somewhere, even though it didn't seem likely to lead to an exclusive photograph of Jim sitting on a beach on the west African coast alive and well.

The official story was that before Bill Siddons went to Paris in answer to Pamela's call, he said he had telephoned the French police to confirm whether the rumours that an American by the name of Jim Morrison had died that weekend were true. His call was made on July 5. He said the police denied any such knowledge and no death of an American fitting the description was recorded. Siddons also drew a blank with the American Embassy. This was why the rumour that Jim was still alive gained credence. I was feeling a lot happier. I could return to England safe in the knowledge that at least the information we had gathered contradicted that published in the press and in the various Morrison biographies.

However, the research wasn't over yet.

Before the Paris trip I was returning home one evening when a radio disc-jockey announced that Oliver Stone, the Hollywood film director of *Wall Street*, *Platoon* and *Salvador*, was due to start work on a film of Jim Morrison's life story. This was a strong factor in going to Paris when I did. However, the impending film could be an advantage or disadvantage. I had to get the story quickly otherwise my exclusive would certainly be uncovered by his researchers.

Once back in Cambridge I set to work writing letters and sending faxes. Filming was to start in March, 1990. Time was now an utmost priority.

CHAPTER THREE

THE END

IT WASN'T UNTIL January 19, 1990, that I received a parcel containing the documents from Père Lachaise at my home in Cambridge. The package contained the burial permit, receipt of purchase (showing Pamela had made the transaction) and the address of the funeral directors.

The burial permit revealed an oddity under the section entitled "Observations" which was hand written and appeared to translate as "shiny shoes and mackintosh or raincoat." Nadine double checked her translation but it came out the same. This appeared to mean that Jim was buried wearing those items of clothing. Weird. I even wondered if this was meant as a message from Jim Morrison. According to Irish folklore, shiny shoes indicate a connection with the spirit world. I thought this figured, considering Morrison's background and occasional dabbling with black magic.

I wrote back to Père Lachaise to establish the meaning of the "Observations" entry because it may have meant that Jim was wearing shiny shoes and a mackintosh at the time of his death, but because he died in the bath this seemed highly unlikely!

Inevitably Père Lachaise did not reply and eventually Nadine had to telephone. They told her that the notes on the "Observations" section were in reality an abbreviated description of the coffin: "Varnished oak lined with water-proof canvas." Nadine was amazed. She looked again at the document and saw where the confusion lay. Some French words were very similar to various French abbreviations. So much for Irish folklore.

On January 18, 1990, I phoned the Morrison family lawyers in Los Angeles and had a brief conversation with Mr. Manion who handled their affairs. I introduced myself in the usual manner and told him that I had been investigating the case for some time.

"What do you mean by case?" he asked.

I explained that I was researching Jim Morrison's last days in Paris and said that I had uncovered a number of peculiarities that might perhaps interest them. I also said I was only prepared to release the information on condition that I receive a letter of authorisation to obtain more documents. He said he would contact the family and ask them but doubted if they would comply.

"The family are unwilling to have any kind of publicity concerning them or their son," he said in a matter of fact way.

I asked if he knew of any police records concerning Jim's death and that Pam had made a false declaration about her relationship to Jim. I thought maybe he did know about this and if so then the facts I had obtained were not so exclusive.

"I do not know, and that is an honest answer," he answered.

Even with that answer it was difficult to determine whether or not he knew all the facts. We exchanged the usual pleasantries. I felt that I had handled the phone call badly to the point that I may have come across as a blackmailer. This I didn't want so that evening I typed a letter to Mr. Manion to try and explain my intentions more clearly. I have always had this problem of not being able to express myself properly. The letter of authorization was something I desperately needed. Without it my research might never be completed. I knew what I wanted to say but, as usual, it came out differently. I suppose it was due to over excitement. Anyway, I sent off the letter.

My next task was to make contact with Danny Sugerman the co-author of *No One Here Gets Out Alive*. I hoped he would put me in touch with certain people who had the last contact with Jim Morrison. Sugerman had been an employee of The Doors, working casually from their offices as a sort of unofficial archivist who collected and pasted up press cuttings and answered fan mail on the group's behalf. He went on to manage Ray Manzarek and still occupies a managerial position within The Doors' hierarchy, handling some of their business affairs, especially those connected with the print media.

One of the characters that I hoped Sugerman would put me in touch with was Jonathan Dolger. He was the editor at Simon & Schuster in New York who received a telegram from Jim on

THE END

July 2, 1971, regarding a cover change for Jim's two books of poetry *The Lords* and *The New Creatures* which were about to be published in a single edition.

I had already tried to contact Dolger by making numerous calls but no-one could remember him or knew where he could now be found. This was someone I really wanted to speak to. The telegram was of particular importance as it may have contained some vital evidence regarding Morrison's state of mind. According to many accounts Jim was apparently quite depressed during his last days in Paris. I had tried to find a record of the telegram in Paris but the files held by the Post Office were moved and likely to have been destroyed after five years. I wanted to verify that Jim actually sent the telegram and not Pamela or someone else.

To the best of my knowledge, apart from Pamela, film technician Alan Ronay and the celebrated Left-Bank school film-director Agnes Varda were the last to see Jim alive, sometime around July 2. I also wanted to locate Bill Siddons to hear his account of what happened when he arrived in Paris. I faxed Sugerman on January 23, explaining who I was and what I wanted to know.

It was also vital to make contact with the funeral directors because they were responsible for the disposal of Jim's body. They would have records of the condition of the body, weight, hair colouring and the clothing in which he was buried.

I wrote to Lieutenant Colonel Galeraud at the headquarters of the Paris Fire Brigade requesting further details and telling him what I had learnt. I felt it was likely he would reply considering how well he had received us when we visited him in Paris. I told him that since we had spoken last, more details had emerged. The police had confirmed they were also involved in this case, and more details from them would be forthcoming. The Medical Institute had confirmed that they were not involved in the matter at all. Therefore, I concluded that no autopsy was performed.

I also informed him that I had unearthed the bizarre story of the police being called to the apartment because of the peculiar smell coming from within it. "In July of 1971, the police were called to Mr. Morrison's apartment after a neighbour had complained about an unpleasant smell," I wrote. "The police

THE
END

were unable to get a response from anyone inside and made the decision to force entry. They then made their way through the apartment to the bathroom whereupon they discovered Mr. Morrison's body in the bathtub. He had obviously been dead for several days. There were also a number of candles and bottles on the bathroom floor."

If this story was true then I could only speculate as to the involvement of the Fire Brigade and that was to assist the police in forcing entry into the apartment. Unless the real story was that the bad smell was from smouldering material ignited in the bathroom by a candle. Because Mr. Morrison was a heavy drinker this left him incapable of getting out of the bathtub and therefore he died from smoke inhalation and lack of oxygen. This meant his death was accidental. Therefore, the Fire Brigade's involvement was to extinguish any potential fire and try to revive Mr. Morrison. This meant that his death would have occurred recently and not happened several days before. His wife Pamela raised the alarm and not a neighbour. Somehow this seemed to fit in with the published date of death better than the version I had described during our meeting at the Fire Station office in Paris.

"I would be grateful for your comments on what I have just disclosed to you," I concluded in the hope of squeezing more information from the Fire Department who, it must be said, had been the most co-operative of my contacts thus far.

I received a reply at the beginning of March. It was very formal and the English had clearly been written by a man unused to the language. It read:

"I have the honour to bring to your knowledge that the rescue of the brigade were called for an 'asphyxie', that they did not smash in any door and had no fire to extinguish. They noted the death of the victim and wrote a true account in keeping with the book you showed me during your recent visit. The rescue were called at 9:21am, arrived at the scene at 9:24am and left the scene at 9:47am."

So the official story was wrong again. The time was different: 9:24am and not 5:00am. This now cast doubts on the death certificate declaration which showed the time of death as 5:00am. Maybe the time of death was merely an estimation made by the doctor. This had to be verified. Could it be

39

THE END

another lie made up by Pamela? The trouble was I couldn't query this with Lieutenant Colonel Galeraud because if there was a discrepancy, the fire brigade might hold an internal inquiry and shut off a potentially valuable source of information. I needed a new source, so I wrote a letter to the Paris Law Courts, approaching them as if I were a journalist checking facts.

I wrote to the Funeral Directors, the Service Municipal des Pompes Funèbres, asking if they had any records concerning Jim Morrison. They should have had documents relating to the preparation and burial of the body. I wanted to know when Pamela first notified them of the death and who paid for their services. I was still keeping an open mind that the whole thing could be a hoax. The funeral directors' records could show that the body they had prepared for burial was that of Morrison and not some other person. The body would have been collected from the apartment and taken to the funeral home to be laid out. I asked for a description of the body: hair colouring, body weight, and condition. The condition of the body was particularly important since it would verify or disprove the story of Mr. Thomas's son that the body had been lying in the bath for several days resulting in decomposition which caused the unpleasant smell to come from the apartment. Could this be the reason for the sealed coffin? What type of coffin was it? Finally, I wanted to know what the funeral arrangements were and if they would send me photo-copies of their files.

There were now a number of letters and faxes out there, and hopefully a great deal of information was due to return. I had to keep the momentum going otherwise the research would stagnate. Would there ever be any concrete evidence to show what really happened to Jim Morrison? This could go on for years. I hoped not.

On February 10, I received a call from the agency in town from where I sent my faxes (at an extortionate rate). They said that a fax had just come in from the States for me. It was from Danny Sugerman.

This was good.

"What does it say?" I asked.

"Sorry Mr. Seymore, but we're not allowed to say unless you

have paid for it," she informed me.

"Oh come on. I'll be round shortly to collect it." The people I have to deal with in this business. She gave in and read it to me over the phone. I laughed. Sugerman had a sense of humour. I felt I already knew him after reading *No One Here Gets Out Alive*. I ran around to pay them their money. His reply read as follows:

> Bob,
> *Usually I send all inquiries and fan letters a form response. Don't worry, seeing as I don't know who you are, however, I can't answer your questions either. Before I attempt to do so, can you tell me:*
>
> *1. Who the hell are you?*
>
> *2. What are you?*
>
> *3. Why are you?*
>
> *4. Just got back from where? Paris, America or the UK? If Paris then it seems to me that without seeing Alan Ronay or Agnes Varda, it was a wasted trip on the Morrison front. Or Hervé Muller, too, for that matter.*
> *I was intrigued by your presumptuous tone in the letter. Is he doing a book I ask myself? An article? Or is he a fan, maybe, very serious? Or is he merely English? Or an American who has successfully integrated the English trait of presumptuousness?*
>
> *Let me know...*
> *Danny.*

Instead of returning to my office I went home and wrote a reply to be faxed straight back to him:

> Danny,
> *Thanks for your fax of 10/02/90. I was beginning to give you up. Difficult questions Danny.*

THE END

41

THE END

1) A question I've often asked myself. I operate a successful commercial and industrial photographic business here in Cambridge which was established 10 years ago. I am also a freelance photojournalist with a reputation to back it up. I am dedicated and determined to follow investigative journalism. It can be like 'flogging a dead horse' at times.

2) I am a 35 year old American without innate breeding and grateful for it. Therefore, I shall always remain an American. I have lived in many countries during my life and arrived in the UK late 1971. A somewhat boring story. I hope to return to the USA one day.

3) I am not responsible for that one.

4) Yes, recently returned from Paris. My interest there was not Alan Ronay or Agnes Varda, although it would be interesting to interview them. Hervé Muller is not on the top of my list. I am aware of his book and its contents. Prefer the pictures. My journey was to clear up the mystery surrounding Jim Morrison's demise. My research is nearing completion but there are a number of details I am still awaiting confirmation on. What I do have however already contradicts what is known in the public domain. I have the documents.

With regard to an article or a book my options are open, but my talents are not for the written word. I appreciate good music and clever lyrics but I do not consider myself a "fan".
I regret the 'English trait of presumptuousness' but you grow to be like the people you live and work with.

Kind regards, Bob.

I still hadn't received a reply from the Morrison lawyers and time was running out. I desperately needed that letter of authorization from the family so I could obtain the various documents from the police and the fire brigade in Paris. The idea of Oliver Stone releasing a film on Jim Morrison which ended with a historically inaccurate account of his death was something I hoped to prevent. Failing that, I could at least publish my version of the story. Timing was crucial. I sent another fax to Mr. Manion. I never did get a reply.

That evening I tried telephoning Danny Sugerman in Los Angeles. Six days had passed since I received his fax and sent my reply and it was now beginning to look as though he wasn't going to answer. The phone rang.

"Hello," the voice on the other end answered.

"Can I speak to Danny Sugerman, please?"

"This is Danny Sugerman," he replied in a rough gravelly voice as though he had been disturbed from a deep sleep and a hard night's smoking.

"Who is it?" he asked.

"It's Bob Seymore calling from England. You may recall I sent you a fax?"

"Oh yeah," he said in the same voice.

"Have I woken you up?" I enquired politely.

"Yeah," he said.

"What's the time there?" I asked.

"9:00 o'clock in the morning."

"I do beg your pardon," I said, grovelling.

"Call me back later," he said as he hung up on me.

A few hours later I tried again. He was out. I assumed the woman I spoke to was his secretary. She told me to hang on and she would patch me through to his car phone. It wasn't exactly a clear line but we were still able to have a conversation. He was willing to answer my questions and apologized for not answering my fax but he didn't really have the time to sit down at a typewriter because of his commitments to forthcoming books and his assistance on the Oliver Stone project. I asked him if he knew where Jonathan Dolger was but he said he hadn't heard from Jonathan in about fifteen years. I asked about Bill Siddons and he told me that he now managed David Crosby and he could be found through Crosby's record label.

"Is there any more information regarding Jim Morrison's death?" I enquired.

"The book *No One Here Gets Out Alive* could have summed up Morrison's death in any form," he said. "Drug overdose,

THE END

43

THE END

was he or wasn't he alive and so on. Jim had a capricious nature. Morrison's death could have involved a number of factors. If you believe in a conspiracy theory, and I don't believe in this at all, you could say that the CIA and other intelligence agencies may have had a hand in the deaths of Hendrix, Janis Joplin and then Morrison. Simply for the reason that they were leaders of a generation during the 1960's and as leaders they had a lot of power."

I asked him if he knew of any police records and fire brigade reports of that time but he couldn't remember. He did say that under the Freedom Of Information Act he saw a number of documents concerning the case. I asked if Danny had seen such documents, then why were there no details of them in any of his books. He said that Pamela had told him things about Jim's death that he promised her he would never divulge.

"Very interesting," I said. Maybe he would tell me what they were?

"Not on your life." But he did suggest that I get a copy of his latest book *Wonderland Avenue* as there was information in it about Jim Morrison that would be useful to me. He asked me to let him know what I had gathered once I completed my research. The conversation ended with my feeling that nothing new had been gained from that line of enquiry.

Since no-one seemed to have any intention of replying to my letters, on the afternoon of February 19 I asked Nadine round to my office to make a number of calls to Paris to follow them up. The Law Court had the police file in their archives but it seemed as if it was going to take at least a month before they would reply. I asked Nadine to tell them that an answer was needed before March 1. This seemed to work and they said they would mark my letter as URGENT! My letter was being passed from one department to another and if you wanted to speak with anyone in particular then they were either out to lunch, on holiday or in a meeting. This was the case with every office we tried.

Monsieur Valley, the man in charge of the funeral directors, was away. We phoned the fire brigade again and spoke with Lieutenant Colonel Galeraud to ascertain the exact time the doctor arrived at the Morrison apartment on July 3, 1971. He was none too pleased to hear from me, in fact he was somewhat pissed off to find I was still plaguing him. He made it clear that he only helped me as a favour and that he could not release any further information as it was confidential. That conversation came to an abrupt end.

It took me a couple of days to locate Bill Siddons, I sent an urgent message to his fax number. I wasn't sure whether the number I had was his office number or that of David Crosby's record company. Either way he would have received it. However, it had to be worded in terms only he would understand, not that it did any good. He never replied. I guess he'd become fed up with people asking him questions about his trip to Paris in July of 1971.

My local fax agency was getting rich and I seemed to be getting nowhere. If the situation didn't improve soon I was going to be in real trouble with nothing concrete to publish. Just pieces of a large puzzle. This research was taking its toll and costing me a great deal of money with no guarantee of recouping what I had spent.

I wasn't entirely in this for the money, however, though my business account overdraft was climbing and I had the usual problems of clients not paying on time. Fortunately I have a very patient and understanding bank manager.

On February 23, Nadine managed to get through to the funeral directors. They confirmed that they had received my letter and said they intended to reply. Monsieur Valley, head of the department was there and told Nadine that Morrison's body had been taken to the Medical Institute for a post-mortem examination. No doubt at all. This was incredible and certainly quite a revelation. The woman at the Medical Institute told me she looked up that name on the computer and it was not registered as having been taken there at all. Why would she lie unless she hadn't bothered to look it up? This seemed the most likely explanation. Monsieur Valley said he was going to the Medical Institute the following week and he would look up the files on Jim Morrison himself. If it turned out that Morrison's body did go to the Institute for an autopsy then this would expose another of Pamela's lies. She was becoming an unreliable witness to the events of 1971.

On February 26 Nadine called Monsieur Valley again. He still insisted that Morrison's body had been taken to the

THE
END

45

**THE
END**

Medical Institute for an autopsy. He still planned to visit the Institute and would ring back with more information the next day. He was true to his word and did return the call. He had looked up the records and Morrison's body did not appear to have had an autopsy. Pamela had not lied after all. I was still running up dead ends.

Monsieur Valley was helpful concerning the funeral arrangements. He told us that the coffin was of varnished oak and measured 1.90 metres in length to contain a body measuring 1.82 to 1.86 metres. It was ordered by an American woman and was delivered to the Morrison apartment where it stayed until the funeral. Unfortunately, Monsieur Valley was unable to tell us when the coffin was actually delivered to the apartment.

His letter arrived sometime in the first week of March and confirmed all that he said on the phone. He added that the original funeral company - Bigot - had ceased trading many years ago and their records were no longer traceable. The funeral took place on July 7 and in addition to the coffin they supplied a hearse and four pallbearers to take the body from 17, rue Beautreillis, in the 4th arrondissement of Paris to Père Lachaise cemetery. No clergy attended.

At this time I still had not read Danny Sugerman's semi-autobiographical book *Wonderland Avenue* which had only recently been published in the UK. As I understood it from the book, Jim was unaware that Pam used heroin. This seems hard to believe but in the early days she only snorted the drug. It was only in the latter stages of her life that she injected it. Pamela Courson died of an overdose April 24, 1974. Sugerman's book describes a time when Morrison snorted heroin by mistake thinking it was cocaine. It almost killed him and he would have died had it not been for the quick thinking of friends who managed to revive him.

Maybe Jim came upon Pam's heroin, thought it was cocaine and snorted it, and that led to his death. Possibly Pam tried to revive him by helping him into the bath and soaking him in cold water. When this didn't work, and it was obvious that he was dead she may have removed Jim's clothing so it would appear he died while taking a bath. She obviously did not want to be arrested in a foreign country for possession of narcotics. It was possible that a doctor's observations would not necessarily show an overdose but only the resulting heart failure. Pam, of course, would deny any use of drugs if asked. There was no evidence to believe otherwise and Pam's friends would naturally seek to protect her. Jim was dead and nothing could bring him back. Hence the conspiracy of silence. It was a theory worth considering.

A few days earlier, Nadine had called Monsieur Thomas in Paris and this time he gave us the name of his neighbour in the same building. He asked us to be discreet about how we got the name. The neighbour was a Monsieur A. Chastagnol. In my letter to him I gave him the usual blurb... American journalist, working in England, researching the death of James Douglas Morrison etc. I told him that I had recently visited his fair city and had discovered that he may have been an eye witness: a neighbour lending a hand to a fellow neighbour in a time of trouble. I explained that since 1971 there had been many stories and countless rumours published concerning Mr. Morrison's last days, most of which were complete untruths or just plain rubbish. I told him I hoped to set the record straight. I told him that I had already uncovered new evidence from official documents that painted an entirely different picture, but it was very slow research. I said that I appreciated that July 3, 1971 was long ago but asked him to remember all he could.

I realized that receiving a reply from Mr. Chastagnol was a slim hope but I had to give it a shot. It was very probable that he, like the rest of the neighbours, was fed-up with being hounded by the press for so long so I was prepared to be disappointed. However, three weeks later I received Monsieur Chastagnol's reply, dated March 20, 1990. I was utterly astonished when Nadine translated its contents as follows:

Dear Sir,
Unfortunately, I am afraid I will not be a great help because I did not know Mr. J. Morrison when he was alive. He was a very 'discreet' neighbour and I did not know he was famous. I only saw him on the day of his death when the police were called and I went up to the flat where he had 'just' died. His girlfriend was not there

THE
END

or at least not in the room where I went to with the police (or firemen, I can't really remember). J Morrison was dead, lying on his back next to his bed, dressed in a 'dressing gown' (house clothes). It was then I was told he had died of a drugs overdose, but I am not in a position to confirm this fact. I very quickly withdrew to my own flat. Here you are. That's all.

Yours sincerely,
A. Chastagnol.

Amazing. Here at last was a communiqué from a witness, not connected with the authorities, who *had seen Morrison's body*, someone who was actually there on the day of his death and at the right time. What was Morrison's body doing dressed and on the floor? What happened to the story of his being in the bath? Why wasn't he on the bed? Where was Pamela? What time of day was it? A dozen new questions sprang to my mind. This was too good to be true, yet there it was in black and white.

I had this vision of Morrison overdosing in the early morning and Pamela discovering him. Perhaps Monsieur Chastagnol was the interpreter for Pam that the fire brigade had told us about? Maybe it was he who called the emergency services?

I was certain my witness had more information to tell me. I couldn't explain the conflict between his letter and the fact that the fire brigade told me they found the body in the bath. Maybe they removed the body from the bath and placed it on the floor for some unknown reason. Why not the bed? I was beginning to doubt the authenticity of the fire brigade report or at least what little they allowed me to know of it. Where was this story going?

There was no alternative but to write again to Monsieur Chastagnol for further explanation and hope that he would be more specific. I wondered what revelations were in store for me this time?

The following day Nadine called the Law Courts to see what the hold-up was this time. She told me that the Law Court's photo-copying department had thirteen pages of text from the police report for me. This was great. This was far more than I had ever expected to get. Not bad for someone without a letter of authorisation. I was getting what I wanted. I had a nagging

Top: Morrison, performing at the Isle of Wight Festival in 1970. *(Barry Plummer)*

Bottom: Morrison, performing in Los Angeles in 1967. *(Pictorial Press)*

The view from the street of rue Beautreillis 17, Jim and Pamela's last home in Paris. Their apartment is on the third floor to the right of this picture.
(Bob Seymore)

The view from the courtyard of rue Beautreillis 17. The apartment is on the third floor to the left of this shot. *(Bob Seymore)*

RÉPUBLIQUE FRANÇAISE

MINISTÈRE DE L'INTÉRIEUR

PREFECTURE DE POLICE

DIRECTION
de la
POLICE JUDICIAIRE

SERVICE

ARSENAL

PROCÈS-VERBAL

Rep. Nº 997

AUDITION DE Melle COURSON
Paméla.

Imp. S T 3202 10-69 Translucide

L'an mil neuf cent soixante **et onze**

le **Trois Juillet**

à **quinze** heure , **quarante**

Nous, MANCHEZ Jacques, O.P.P

Officier de Police Judiciaire,

Entendons mademoiselle COURSON
Paméla Susan née le 22 Décembre 1946 à Weed (Californie),sans profession de nationalité Américaine
domiciliée 17 rue Beautreillis à Paris 4e,
elle déclare sur interpellation
"Je suis l'amie de Monsieur MORRISON James et je vis maritalement avec lui depuis 5 ans.

"Je suis arrivé en France avec
mon ami au mois de Mars dernier j'avais trouvé lors
d'un précédent court séjour une sous location à l'adresse 17 rue Beautreillis au 3e étage coté droit.
Mon ami était écrivain mais il viv ait surtout sur
une fortune personnelle.

"Avant de venit habiter rue Beautreillis j'ai vécu 3 semaines avec mon ami à l'Hotel
de Nice rue des Beaux Arts je crois et là mon ami
s'est trouvé souffrant il se plaignait de mal respirer il avait aussi des crises de toux dans la lnuit.
J'avais appelé un médecin ce praticien est venu à l'
Hotel il a prescrit des pilules contre l'asthme;mais
mon ami n'aimait pas voir les med cins et ne s'est
jamais soigné sérieusement.SI Je ne puis préciser
quel est le médecin qui a soigné mon ami et je n'ai
pas gardé d'ordonnance.Lors d'un précédent séjour à
Londres mon ami avait déjà eu les mêmes malaises .

"H er soir j'ai diné avec mon ami
je m'explique mal ,je n'ai pas diné Bier soir et mon
ami est allé seul diner dans un restaurant sans doute dans le quartier.Lorsque mon ami est revenu du re
taurant nous sommes allés tous deux au cinéma voir
jouer "La Vallée de la Peur",le cinéma se trouve près
du métro Le Pelletier il s'appelle je crois "Action
La ayette"?Nous sommes revenus du cinéma vers I heu
re Ce jour ,j'ai fait la vaisselle et mon ami a projeté des films d'amateur avec sa caméra.Mon ami paraissait en bonne santé il semblait très heureux.Mai
je dois dire que mon ami ne se plaignait jamais ce
n'était pas dans sa nature.Ensuite nous avons écouté
des disques je dois dire que le tourne disques se
trouve dans la chambre à coucher et nous écoutions
la muqique allongés tous deux sur le lit.Je crois
que nous nous sommes endormis vers 2h30 mais je ne
puis dire exactement l'electrophone s'arrête automa
tiquement.

SI Non nous n'avons pas eu de rapport sexuel hier soir.

Vers 3het demi je crois car il n'
y a pas de pendule dans la chambre et je ne me suis
pas inquitée de l'heure j'ai été réveillée par le
bruit que faisais mon ami en respirant sa respiratior
était bryyante et j'avais l'impression qu'il étouffa:
cela faisait du bruit j'ai secoué mon ami et je lui
ai envyé quelques giffles pour essayer de le réveil-

..·/··₄

A facsimile of Pamela Courson's statement, given to the French Police in Paris on
July 3, 1971, the most complete factual account of Jim Morrison's final hours in
existence.

RÉPUBLIQUE FRANÇAISE

MINISTÈRE DE L'INTÉRIEUR

PRÉFECTURE DE POLICE

DIRECTION
de la
POLICE JUDICIAIRE

SERVICE

ARSENAL

PROCÈS-VERBAL

Rep. N° 99 7

AUDITION DE Melle
COURSON (suite)

Imp. 5 T 3202 10-69 Translucide

L'an mil neuf cent soixante **et onze**

le **Trois Juillet**

à **seize** heure **trente**

Nous, MANCHEZ Jacques, O.P.P

Officier de Police Judiciaire,

..../..
je l'ai secoué.Il s'est réveillé je lui ai demandé
ce qui n'allait pas,je voulais appeler un médecin.
Mon ami m'a dit qu'il se sentait bien et qu'il ne
voulait pas voir de médecin.Il s'est levé et a mar-
ché dans la chambre puis il m'a dit qu'il voulait
prendre un bain chaud,il s'est dirigé vers la salle
de bain il a fait couler son bain alors qu'il se
trouvait dans la baignoire mon ami m'a appelé me
disant qu'il avait la nausée et envie de vomir.Je
suis allée dans la salle de bain en passant j'ai p
pris dans la cuisine un récipient genre marmite de
couleur orange mon ami a vomi dans ce récipient que
je tenais de la nourriture il me semble qu'il y avai
du sang avec,j'ai vidé le contenu,puis de nouveau
mon ami a vomi dans ce récipient uniquement du sang,
puis une troisième fois des caillots de sang.J'ai
vidé à chaque fois le contenu dans le lavabo de la
salle de bain puis j'ai rincé ce récipient. Puis mon
ami m'a dit qu'il se sentait "bizarre",mais il m'a
dit je ne suis pas malad n'appelle pas un médecin
je me sens mieux,c'est fini.Il m'a dit "va te coucher",qu'il allait terminer de prendre son bain et
qu'il viendrait me rejoindre au lit. A ce moment il
me semblait que mon ami allait mieux parce qu'il
avait vomi ses coule rs étaient revenues un peu.Je
suis allée me recoucher et je me suis tout de suite
endormie j'était rassurée.
          Je ne sais combien de temps j'ai
pu dormir,je me suis réveillée en sursaut et j'ai
vu que mon ami n'était pas couché près de moi j'ai
couru à la salle de bain et j'ai vu que mon ami
était encore dans la baignoire sa tête n'était pas
dans l'eau il semblait dormir sa tête était appuyée
contre le rebord de la baignoire,un peu de sang se
trouvait sous les narines.J'ai secoué mon ami j'ai
cru pouvoir le réveiller,je croyais qu'il avait un
malaise et qu'il était inconscient.J'ai essayé de
le sortir de la baignoire mais je n'ai pas pu.A ce
moment j'ai téléphoné à Monsieur RONAY un compatrio-
te pour qu'il appelle une ambulance. Puis une demi
heure après environ Monsieur RONAY est venu chez moi.
Lorsque Monsieur RONAY est arrivé avec son amie Ma
dame Anièce DEMY ils ont appelé je crois les pompier
ou la Police.
          SI Je suis domiciolée aux USA à
l'adresse suivante 8216 Norton Avenue Los Angelès
Californie,ma soeur est domiciliée à cette adresse
et habituellement je vis chez ma soeur.
          Je vais m'occuper des obsèques avec
l'aide de mon ami Monsieur RONAY.
          Mademoiselle COURSON ne parlant pas
Fra,çais,lecture est faite par Monsieur NORAY qui
nous a servi d'interprète. Melle COURSON persiste et
signe. L'O.P.J

REPUBLIQUE FRANÇAISE.

MINISTÈRE DE L'INTÉRIEUR

PREFECTURE DE POLICE

DIRECTION
de la
POLICE JUDICIAIRE

SERVICE

ARSENAL

PROCÈS-VERBAL

Rep. N° 997

AUDITION DE Mr RAISSON
Alain

eutenant des sapeurs
.mpiers).

L'an mil neuf cent soixante **et onze**

le **Trois Juillet**

'à **quatorze trente**   heure

Nous, **MANCHEZ** Jacques,O.P.P

Officier de Police Judiciaire,

Entendons Monsieur RAISSON Alain
né le IO Octobre 1940 à Paris 8e,Lieutenant,à la Briga
de des Sapeurs Pompiers de Paris ,7 rue de évigné à
Paris 4e,

il déclare,
"Ce matin à 9h20 je me suis rendu
chef de garde du fourgon pompe I7 rue Beautreillis à
Paris 4e au 3e étage droite.,pour axphyxié.En arivant
sur place la porte de l'appartement nous a été ouverte
par une jeune femme ne parlant pas Français qui nous
a e mmené dans la salle de bain.Dans cette pièce se
trouvait,dans la baignoire un homme entierement nu de
frote corpulence.La têtense trouvait hors de l'eau re-
posant sur la paillasse droit rejetée en arrière.La bai
gnoire était pleine d'eau legerement teinté rosé le
bras droit reposait sur le rebord de la baignæbre dont
l'eau était encore tiède,ainsi que le corps.Avec mes
hommes j'ai sorti le corps et je l'ai étendu par terre
dans la chambre à coucher où j'ai commencé à pratiquer
massages cardiaques mais je me suis rendu compte aussi-
tot de la mort certaine de la victime j'ai fait déposer
le corps sur le lit.
SI Lorsque je suis entré dans la
salle d'eau il y avait un,peu d'eau à terre près de la
baignoire et le peignoir de la personne qui nous a ou-
vert la porte était mouillé.
SI Un peu de sang a coulé de la na
rine droite lorsque nous avons étendu le corps par terre.

Après avoir lu persiste et signe
L'Officier de Police Judiciaire

A facsimile of the statement of Alain Raisson, of the Paris Fire Department, the
first French official to see Morrison's body after Pamela alerted the authorities.

DIRECTION DU CABINET

Mairies de Paris

MANDAT D'INHUMATION

RENSEIGNEMENTS DIVERS

Décès déclaré le 3/7/71 à 14 heures

Lieu du service religieux ____

2 e Classe. Taxe 12 fr.

Exposition à __X__ heures

OBSERVATIONS

Imp. Chambord 30.000 3/69 Cde 10255

M. C. 228

RÉPUBLIQUE FRANÇAISE
LIBERTÉ · ÉGALITÉ · FRATERNITÉ

PRÉFECTURE DE PARIS

MAIRIE DU 4 e ARRONDISSEMENT DE LA VILLE DE PARIS

Le Maire du ____ e Arrondissement,

Vu le certificat remis par Monsieur ____ docteur en médecine,

Et qui constate le décès de Monsieur ____ DOUGLAS MORRISON

Agé de 27 ans, arrivé le ____ à ____ heures

Rue Beautreillis n° 17

Quartier

Ordonne au Chef de convoi (après avoir fait mettre le corps dans un cercueil muni d'une estampille portant

le n° 611 (s) de faire transporter et inhumer le corps au cimetière de ____

le ____ 19 ____ à ____ heures 80

Paris, le 6 ____ 19 ____

2e Lot T. N° 1540

A facsimile of Morrison's medical report, prepared by Dr Max Vassille in Paris on
July 3, 1971.

Jim Morrison's grave at Père Lachaise Cemetery near Paris. *(Bob Seymore)*

doubt, however, that the information was going to be just a pile of useless press cuttings. However, Nadine had more to report.

"There's a catch," she said.

"Oh no! Now what?" I asked.

"You must pay for the information to cover the cost of photocopies before they can send them," Nadine said. "They will send you the invoice first and then you send the payment and they will post the documents to you."

"You're kidding?" I replied in disbelief. "Why in the hell didn't they tell me this in the first place?"

Nadine just shook her head unable to offer an explanation. I could see further delays piling up, but Nadine had a solution. She phoned them back and said arrangements would be made to have the copies paid for and collected by our representative. This was a friend of Nadine's and sure enough, a couple of days later her friend phoned to say she had the documents. But that there was a hitch. The postal service in Paris was on strike.

Nadine waited for my exclamations of disbelief and swearing to die down, then reassured me, "Don't worry, my friend will send everything by special delivery; a service that is unconnected with the strike."

"Phew! That was close."

The next few days were difficult. I became even more irritable and snappy each day as I waited for the morning post to arrive. Then, on Monday April 2, 1990, a large white envelope marked "Special Delivery" was waiting among my other mail. I clutched the envelope to my chest and smiled with relief. I phoned Nadine and went straight round to her house to have the thirteen pages translated on the spot. They turned out to be a remarkable series of documents, describing in some detail Jim's movements the day before he died, right up until his last hour alive. Certain details were so clearly described that I could visualize him. For those brief moments during Nadine's translation Jim Morrison was alive for me and I was privileged to be watching his every movement. I was the proverbial fly on the wall.

Poor Jim, he was really ill. I was amazed that no-one had cared enough for him to insist that he seek medical help long before he died. Jim certainly had a laissez-faire attitude towards his health and was never keen on seeing doctors, but

THE
END

49

THE END

all the evidence pointed towards the fact that he was a very sick man indeed, and this would have been obvious to any of his friends in Paris.

It was incredible. The existence of these documents had always been denied but here they were, thirteen pages which had been locked in a time capsule and which described everything. Unfortunately, I now had to admit beyond doubt that Jim was dead. I wanted to hold on to the dream that he was alive and that there was still a chance of confronting a very clever man. Now the dream was dead too. There it was. A signed statement made by Jim's girlfriend Pamela Courson and Alan Ronay.

I just couldn't understand their reasons for denying that there was a police record, fire brigade report, and a doctor's report. Pam and Alan's statements made interesting reading. I kept asking myself why Pam didn't do something before it was too late? She might have been able to save Jim's life. The statements were full of "if onlys."

The doctor's report was written by Dr. Max Vassille and it seemed very dubious to me. It was vague, attributed Jim's death to natural causes and just skimmed over his underlying health problems without investigating them at all. There was nothing natural about Jim's death. There should have been a post-mortem examination. Later, I double checked in writing with the Medical Institute to see if there had been an autopsy under the name James Douglas Morrison giving all the relevant details. A letter came back confirming that no person of that name, date or place was registered on their computer before or after the month described in my letter. After reading the file I was astonished that the authorities did not investigate the case more thoroughly because the statements often contradicted each other and depended so much on Pamela's testimony. However, Pam is dead; her lips are sealed - and her friends aren't telling either.

CHAPTER FOUR

THE PAGES THAT follow consist primarily of the entire police file concerning the death of Jim Morrison in its original state, followed by the translation and a few comments from me. It proves beyond any doubt whatsoever that Jim Morrison did die on July 3, 1971, at the Paris apartment he shared with Pamela Courson and discredits once and for all any wild stories - or hopes - about his having faked his death in order to escape celebrity or imprisonment or both. Here are the records and statements which for reasons unknown (and by persons unknown) have been kept under wraps since 1971.

The dossier opens with an account of the scene as reported by Lieutenant Alain Raisson of the Paris fire brigade to the Police Criminal Investigations Department on July 3, 1971 at 2:30pm. The report begins with the officer's name, date and place of birth, rank, and place of service in Paris. This is followed by a transcript of his verbal report:

"This morning at 9:20am I went as commander of my unit to 17 rue Beautreillis, Paris 4th, the third floor, right hand side flat in answer to a report of 'asphyxiation'. When we reached the flat, the door was opened by a young woman who could not speak French and who took us to the bathroom. In this room there was a man in the bath, completely naked and heavily built. His head was above the water, resting on the edge of the bath. The bath was full of water, slightly pink in colour and his right arm was resting on the side of the bath. The water was still lukewarm, as well as the body. Together with my men, I took the body out and laid it on the floor of the bedroom where I started giving heart massage but I immediately realized that the victim was dead and I had the body

placed on the bed.

"(N.B.:When I went into the bathroom, there was some water on the floor beside the bath and the dressing gown of the person who opened the door to us was wet.)

"(N.B.:A little blood ran down from his right nostril when we laid the body on the floor.)

"(signed) Manchez, Jacques,

(signed) Raisson, Alain."

This report tallied with my letter from the fire brigade stating that they had received the emergency call at 9:21am, arrived at the flat at 9:24am and departed from there at 9:47am. The term 'asphyxiation' could refer to a number of serious situations: choking, suffocation or breathing difficulties (but not drowning). In situations such as these the fire brigade "resuscitation unit" responds to the emergency.

I would have thought, however, that if Jim had died at 5:00am, as we have been led to believe, then the bathwater would have been cold. However, the water is reported as being lukewarm as well as the body. This would suggest that Jim took a bath later than 5:00am and that his death occurred later than supposed. Monsieur Chastagnol must have entered the room before Jim's body was placed on the bed but there is no mention of this in the report. Chastagnol insisted that the body was clothed.

The description of Pam's wet clothing verifies Pam's story that she tried to get Jim out of the bath. She must have splashed water around quite a bit. The fact that it was her dressing gown that was wet also suggests that she was not long out of bed.

The next to arrive at the apartment were the police whose report to the State Prosecutor was dated July 4, 1971, and written by Police Superintendent, Mr. Robert Berry. It read as follows:

"I have the honour to send a diligent account of proceedings according to my investigation concerning the death of the named: MORRISON, James Douglas, born on 8th December, 1943, at Clearwater (Florida, U.S.A.), an American writer living since March 1971 at 17 rue

THE END

Beautreillis, Paris 4th Arrondissement, Home address 851a Santa Monica Blvd. Los Angeles (California) 90069.

"On July 3rd between 8:30am and 9:00am Miss Pamela COURSON - Mr. MORRISON's concubine - noticed that her boy friend who had got up in the middle of the night, apparently around 4 o'clock in order to have a bath, had not returned to bed. Miss COURSON went to the bathroom and saw that Mr. MORRISON was in the bath unconscious, with his head above the water and resting on the side of the bath. Miss COURSON, who does not speak French, telephoned a couple of compatriots and friends, Mr. RONAY and his girlfriend Miss DEMY, temporarily in Paris at 86 rue Daguerre, who came straight away and called the Fire Brigade and Police.

"The Fire Brigade men took Mr. MORRISON's body out of the bath, the water of which was still lukewarm, and tried to massage his heart, without any success. Enquiries brought to light that Mr. MORRISON had been feeling faint in the middle of the night; according to his concubine he was breathing with difficulty and decided to have a hot bath. According to Miss COURSON's statement he started vomiting and she collected this vomit in a container which she rinsed afterwards before going back to bed, thinking that the vomiting would have helped and that he would return to bed after his bath. She went back to sleep. Nothing suspicious was noticed on the spot either in the flat or on the body, which bore no trace of blows, lesions or needle marks.

"Dr. Vassille conducted the medical examination and concluded that death was by natural causes due to heart failure, which could have been caused by a change of temperature, following a bath, causing the classical "myocardial infarction", a case of sudden death.

"It is significant that Mr. RONAY and Miss COURSON had already noticed that Mr. MORRISON had been suffering from respiratory problems for several months and that he looked unwell. Despite the advice given to him, Mr. MORRISON had always refused to see a doctor.

Consequently, I submit your burial certificate. The body is at 17, rue Beautreillis. Miss COURSON and Mr. RONAY wish to organize the funeral arrangements.

The Superintendent,
R. Berry."

The term "concubine" is used by the French as a legal definition for a live-in-lover who has the same rights as a wife. As a legal term the word has none of the derogatory implications it has in English.

I was surprised that Pamela decided that he should be buried in France. Jim may have been opposed to many of the things America stood for at the time but he was also quoted as saying, "I am primarily an American; second, a Californian; third, a resident of Los Angeles."

July 3 must have been a long, tiring, busy and stressful day for Pamela and Alan Ronay. Among other things, they were required to make a statement at the 4th Arrondissement police station. Pam began giving her account at 3:40pm, translated by Alan Ronay, and did not finish until sometime after 6:40pm. It must have been a harrowing three hours for her. The times are clearly indicated on the report. Pamela gave her statement to Police Officer Jacques Manchez. In it she identifies herself as Pamela Susan COURSON, born 22nd December 1946 at Weed, California. An unemployed American, living at 17 rue Beautreillis, Paris 4th. Her statement read:

"I am Mr. MORRISON's girlfriend and have been living with him for five years. Last March, I came to France with my friend. During a previous short stay I had found rented accommodation at the address 17 rue Beautreillis, third floor, right hand side. My boyfriend was a writer but mostly he lived on a personal fortune.

"Before living at rue Beautreillis, my boyfriend and I lived for three weeks at the Hôtel de Nice, rue des Beaux Arts, I think, and while we were there my friend was sick, he was complaining of difficulty in breathing and he also had coughing fits at night. I called a doctor to the hotel who prescribed pills for asthma but my friend didn't like

55

THE END

to see doctors and never looked after himself seriously.

"(N.B.: I cannot say precisely who the doctor was, and I didn't keep the prescription. During a previous stay in London, my friend had already experienced the same problems.)

"Last night I had dinner with my friend... I am not explaining myself properly - I didn't have dinner last night, my friend went out to a restaurant on his own, probably in the area. When my friend came back from the restaurant, we both went to the cinema to see the film Death Valley. The cinema is beside the Metro Station Le Pelletier, I think it is called Action Lafayette. We came back from the cinema around 1:00am, I did the dishes and my friend watched an amateur film from a projector. My friend looked in good health, he seemed very happy. However, I have to say, my friend never used to complain, it wasn't in his nature. We then listened to records; I should say that the record player is in the bedroom and we were both listening to the music lying on the bed. I think we went to sleep at 2:30am approximately, but I can't say exactly because the record player stops automatically.

"(N.B.: No, we didn't have any sexual intercourse last night.)

"Round about 3:30am I think, because there was not a clock in the bedroom and I didn't notice the time, I was woken by the noise my friend was making with his breathing. His breathing was noisy and I thought he was choking. It was noisy. I shook my friend, I slapped him a few times to wake him, I shook him and he woke up. I asked him what was wrong, I wanted to call a doctor. He got up, walked about in the bedroom and then told me he wanted to have a bath. He headed towards the bathroom and ran his bath. When he was in the bath he called me and said that he felt sick and felt like vomiting. On my way I picked up an orange coloured bowl. He vomited food into the bowl I was holding, I think there was blood in it. I emptied the contents then my friend vomited into the container again, only blood this time and then a third time blood clots. Each time I emptied the bowl down the *wash basin of the bathroom, then I washed the bowl. My friend then told me he felt strange but he said, "I don't feel sick, don't call a doctor, I feel better. It's over!" He told me to "go to bed" and said that he was going to finish his bath and would join me in bed. At this time it appeared to me that my friend felt better because he had vomited and his colour had returned a bit. I went back to bed and I immediately fell asleep. I was reassured.*

"I don't know how long I slept. I awoke with a start and I saw that my friend wasn't lying next to me. I ran to the bathroom and saw that my friend was still in the bath, a little blood was running from his nostril. I shook my friend, thinking he would wake up. I thought he had fainted and was unconscious. I tried to get him out of the bath but I couldn't. Then I phoned up Mr. RONAY. He came with his girlfriend, Miss Agnes DEMY, and they called, I think, the Fire Brigade or the Police.

"(N.B. I live in the U.S.A. at the following address - 8216 Norton Avenue, Los Angeles, California. My sister lives at the same address and normally I live at my sister's. I am going to organize the funeral arrangements with Mr. RONAY's help.

Miss COURSON does not speak French so Mr. RONAY has been acting as an interpreter.)

"(Signed),
PAMELA COURSON".

Alan Ronay made his statement to Police Officer Jacques Manchez of the Criminal Investigations Department at 6:50 in the evening of the same day, 3rd July, 1971, following straight on from Pamela. First Mr. Ronay gave his particulars: born 16th June, 1933, at Neuilly (Seine), a Cinema Technician, of American nationality, living temporarily at 86, rue Daguerre, Paris and usually at 14527 Dickens Avenue, Los Angeles, (California). He stated:

"I have known Mr. MORRISON since 1963, he was one of my friends. Mr. MORRISON came to see me in London on the 5th June last month, when I was on holiday there. He was with Miss COURSON. I knew that my friend had

THE END

THE
END

been living with Miss COURSON for several years.

"This morning around 8:30am, I was woken by a telephone call from Miss COURSON asking for help. She asked me to come at once, she was crying. She told me that her friend was unconscious. I got up and went straight to rue Beautreillis with my girlfriend, Miss DEMY. When I arrived I saw the firemen in the street and asked them what was going on but they didn't tell me. I went up to the flat and saw Miss COURSON who was crying and who told me that her friend was dead. I refused to see the body but I know that when I arrived he was already on his bed, out of the bath.

"(N.B.:- My friend MORRISON was a heavy drinker but he couldn't really take alcohol.)

"(N.B. I am sure that my friend didn't use drugs. He often talked about how foolish it was of young people to take drugs and regarded this as a very serious problem.)

"I was with Mr. MORRISON, the whole of yesterday afternoon and I left him around 6:00pm. I thought he looked unwell and I told him. He said that everything was fine. As a matter of fact, he never used to complain. I went for a walk with him yesterday afternoon, he told me he felt tired. During the walk he had a fit of hiccups. It seems to me this fit lasted about an hour. At one point he closed his eyes and I thought his complexion looked grey. He told me he was closing his eyes in order to concentrate and get rid of the hiccups. We also took some logs up to the flat from the courtyard. My friend struggled. It was an effort for him.

"I am going to organize the funeral arrangements with Miss COURSON.

"(Signed) Jacques Manchez,
(Signed) Alan Ronay."

According to the statement made by police officer Jacques Manchez, Mr. Ronay stated verbally that he had phoned the emergency services when he arrived at the flat and saw Morrison in the bath. He said this on the morning of the 3rd, at 9:40am. This contradicts the statement he made at the police station when he had said that he never saw the body and that the fire brigade were already at the apartment. It seemed strange that the police didn't pick up on this point. He either called the fire brigade or he didn't.

Next came a statement from police officer Jacques Manchez of the Arsenal Police Station made July 3rd, 1971, at 9:40am. He states:

"We are informed by the local police that the police emergency services bus of the 4th District went today at 9:25am to 17 rue Beautreillis in Paris 4th Arrondissement, staircase A, third floor flat on the right hand side. The tenant of the flat, Mr. MORRISON, James aged 28, was found dead in his bath by his concubine, Miss COURSON, Pamela.

"We are reporting to the head of department who has asked us to proceed with an enquiry.

"(Signed),
Jacques Manchez,
Police Officer."

"We are going to 17 rue Beautreillis in Paris 4th Arrondissement, Staircase A, third floor flat on the right hand side. At the scene we note the presence of firemen from the Sevigne Brigade and the Police Emergency Services bus of the 4th Arrondissement.

"The fire chief informs us that he took the body of Mr. MORRISON, the tenant of the flat, from the bath, and that his body was placed on the bed in the bedroom after having tried, without success, to resuscitate him by heart massage.

"We then go to the bedroom where we find the body of a young man, quite heavily built, lying on the bed. The body is covered with a bedspread which we removed; he is lying on his back, completely naked, with his arms by his sides. His eyes are half closed and his mouth is slightly open, a trickle of blood coming from his right nostril and his left nostril obstructed by a clot. The body is still supple and bears no trace of traumatism or lesions of any kind.

"We do not notice any signs of disorder in the room

THE END

59

where we are. Continuing on with our observations we go to the bathroom where we find the bath in which Mr. MORRISON's body lay before it was taken to the bed by the firemen. This room is connected with the bedroom by a secondary corridor which also leads to the kitchen. The bath is situated on the left hand side in front of a bidet, on the right hand side there is a wash hand basin and a little cabinet. The outside dimensions of the bath are 1 metre 50 x 65 centimetres, inside the bath there is still some slightly pink coloured water. The bath is 35cms. deep and the water is 19cms. deep. The water is still lukewarm. On the floor next to the cabinet we notice a container, yellow/orange in colour and empty. We leave this room to go to the lounge where we find three people, two women and a man, they are all American; a policeman tells us that it is Pamela COURSON, Mr. MORRISON's girlfriend with whom he lived, Mr.Alan RONAY, compatriot and friend of the MORRISON-COURSON couple and Miss Agnes DEMY, Mr. RONAY's concubine.

"In questioning Mr. RONAY, who is the only one to speak French, he tells us verbally, that this morning between 8:30 and 9:00am, he doesn't know exactly, he received a call at his home, 86, rue Daguerre, Paris 14th, from Miss COURSON asking him to come straight away as her friend MORRISON had fainted in the bath and that she could not call the doctor herself as she was unable to speak French. Mr. RONAY came immediately, accompanied by his girlfriend, Miss DEMY and when he saw his friend MORRISON unconscious in the bath, he called the fire brigade.

"Through Mr. RONAY, Miss COURSON tells us that her friend got up this morning around about 4:00am to have a bath because he was not feeling well. Miss COURSON had gone back to sleep and when she woke around about 8:30am she realized that her friend had not come back to bed. She had then gone to the bathroom and seen her friend unconscious in the bath

with his head outside the water. She had tried to take him out of the bath but couldn't do it because of Mr. MORRISON's height (1 metre 86).

"We request Miss COURSON and Mr. RONAY to attend a hearing.

"(Signed),
Police Officer
Jacques Manchez."

Why was there a delay in calling the emergency services? It was more practical to phone them as soon as he received the call from Pam. It is quite a distance from Ronay's place to Morrison's apartment and the journey could have taken half an hour, if not longer. It is possible that Jim was still barely alive before the emergency services arrived, in which case the delay in calling the emergency services contributed to his death. Did Ronay see the body before calling the fire brigade? We don't know.

On July 3, 1971, at 6:40pm, police officer Jacques Manchez prepared a final document: The Medical Report. It states:

"We record that the Doctor Max VASSILLE, Forensic Doctor, requested by us to examine the body of Mr. MORRISON, after having taken an oath, has given us a Medical Report stating that the death was natural due to heart failure. Please find enclosed, the Medical Report.

"(Signed),
Jacques Manchez,
Police Officer."

"This is to state that the Death Certificate was prepared at the Town Hall of the 4th Arrondissement.

"(Signed),
Jacques Manchez,
Police Officer."

"This is to state that we have identified the deceased from his passport which was given to us by Miss COURSON. James Douglas MORRISON, born on December 8th 1943, Florida (U.S.A.). Passport issued 7th August 1968, valid for three years. We report that

61

THE END

the place of birth of the above named was given to us by Miss COURSON since the information did not appear on the document. We could not get any further information regarding the next of kin.

"(Signed),
Jacques Manchez,
Police Officer."

"We notify the State Prosecutor by telegram, also the Head of the C.I.D.
"(Signed),
Jacques Manchez,
Police Officer."

The police, of course, used Agnes Varda's married name, "Demy" in their reports, which accounts for that difference. I thought that the business with the passport was particularly interesting because Jim is supposed to have lost his original passport, wallet, and driver's licence on a trip to Corsica during the second week of May 1971. Both he and Pam had to return to Paris where Jim had to apply for a new one at the American Embassy. The new passport would have a new date of issue as well as a new expiry date. If Pamela gave them Jim's old passport, I would like to have seen whose picture was in it. The person in the photograph and the person dead on the bed may have been the same, but were they both Jim Morrison? Why didn't she give the police the new passport or was Jim actually using it? This suggested a whole lot of new questions, to say the least.

Next we have the Medical Report compiled and written by Dr. Max Vassille. It states:

"I, the undersigned, Max VASSILLE, qualified as a Doctor by the Paris Medical University, living at Paris, 31 rue du Renard, requested by Mr. BERRY, Robert, Superintendent of the Arsenal District Police. Acting on behalf of the State Prosecutor in accordance with the Article 74 of the Penal Procedures Code, after having promised to give my opinion after taking the oath, I went on the 3rd July 1971 at 6:00pm to 17 rue Beautreillis,

THE END

staircase A 3rd floor on the right in order to examine the body, identified by the Judicial Enquiry as being that of the named, MORRISON, James, aged 28.

"I note: That the body does not show, apart from the lividity of death, any signs of suspicious traumatism or lesions of any kind. A little blood round the nostrils. The history of Mr. MORRISON's condition, such as it was described to us by a friend present at the scene, can be summed up as follows:

"Mr. MORRISON had been complaining for a few weeks of chest pains with dyspnoea; it is evidently coronary problems, possibly aggravated by excessive drinking. One can imagine that on the occasion of a change of outside temperature, followed by a bath, these troubles were suddenly aggravated, leading to classical Myocardial Infarction, causing sudden death.

I conclude from my examination that death was caused by heart failure (natural death).
Paris, 3rd July 1971.
"(Signed),
Max Vassille."

So here we have it, a simple case of natural death. The Doctor ignores the fact that Morrison had some internal haemorrhage and Pamela's evidence that Jim had vomited up blood clots. He ignores the fact there was blood around his nostrils. I decided I would get the opinion of a qualified pathologist and see how natural he thought it was.

From the Police statement it would appear that they notified the Town Hall and registered Jim Morrison's death. The death certificate clearly states that the time of death was 5:00am. Their choice of this time is based on Pamela Courson's testimony. This means it is an estimated time and not based on medical fact. It has already been established that Jim was alive between 4:00 and 5:00am. The doctor did not examine the body until 6:00pm. I understand that French police procedure requires that a doctor from that area examines the corpse within six hours. I can not understand why this wasn't done earlier. Any possible suspects could remove traces of narcotics and tamper with all manner of vital medical evidence. There is no indication that the police saw anything suspicious and no search was carried out at the scene. As far as the Authorities were concerned, it was a straightforward natural death. No more, no less.

I don't buy it. I think there was something seriously wrong with Jim and nothing was done to help him. I think Pamela and his other friends were negligent in their responsibilities. The warning signs were all there. Jim was still young enough to change his habits and rehabilitate himself. He knew this-which is why he had dry periods.

Not only that, Jim Morrison's death could have been caused by an overdose of narcotics. The police doctor did not do a thorough investigation. The information about the circumstances of his death is based entirely on the testimony of Pamela Courson and she was not going to inform the police that she was snorting heroin and that maybe Jim took some, accidentally or otherwise. I regard her testimony as questionable and I think that the Police enquiry was not good enough. I therefore decided to do what I could do to uncover the true circumstances of the death of Jim Morrison.

CHAPTER FIVE

FROM THE EVIDENCE I had gathered since visiting Paris and harassing the authorities into releasing documents, it was now possible to piece together the true story of the final days of Jim Morrison, *The End:*

On Friday, July 2, 1971, Jim probably left the flat around lunchtime to send a telegram to Jonathan Dolger in New York, requesting a change to the cover of his book of poetry *The Lords* and *The New Creatures.* He was unwilling for the publishers to exploit his pop star persona on the book's cover, preferring the book to be marketed in its own right as a book of recent poetry by a newly discovered but relatively anonymous Californian poet and not by the lead singer of the chart topping rock band The Doors. Some hope. If the marketing men had their way, the book of poems would carry on its cover the most ruggedly handsome picture of Jim they could find, preferably a shot from the famous Joel Brodsky sessions in which a fluffy haired Jim was naked from the waist up apart from his necklace of Indian beads.

Some time later he met up with Alan Ronay and they took a walk. It was the beginning of July and it was a warm sunny day. They probably stopped at various sidewalk cafés and walked around taking in the sights. Alan thought Jim was looking unwell and tired. Jim even had a severe fit of hiccups lasting for about an hour. Eventually, they returned to Jim's flat, picked up some logs from the courtyard and took them upstairs. Jim found it a strain to carry them and had to struggle to climb the stairs to the third floor. It's not clear when Alan went home that evening.

According to Pam, Jim ate out alone that evening which would have been some time around 7:30 and 8:00pm. Since he was eating by himself, he probably ate at a local restaurant. He returned to the apartment and he and Pam went to the cinema where they saw the late evening screening of *Death Valley* at around 11:00pm. After the film they returned home. It was now about 1:00am Saturday, July 3. Pam went into the kitchen and washed up some dishes while Jim got out his movie projector and watched a home movie, probably some of the concert footage of The Doors that he brought with him to Paris. According to Pam, Jim looked well. They were both feeling quite content and happy. They went to bed and put a few records on the record-player in their bedroom. They didn't have sex and gradually drifted off to sleep. The time now was 2:30am.

An hour or so later, Pam was woken up by a terrible choking or gurgling noise made by Jim. She thought for a moment that he was choking and tried to arouse him by shaking him and slapping him round the face. This worked and Jim finally woke up. Pam asked him what was wrong. Her first impulse was to call a doctor so it must have been pretty bad. Jim got out of bed and walked around the bedroom. He obviously felt strange and decided to take a bath, thinking it might refresh him or otherwise make him feel better.

He ran a bath, but as soon as he climbed in he called out to Pam that he felt sick and was going to vomit. Pam grabbed an orange coloured bowl and ran down the short corridor to the bathroom. She knelt beside the bath next to Jim and held the bowl under his chin while he threw up. Pam noticed that there was blood mixed in with the vomit. She washed out the bowl in the hand basin but then Jim began to vomit again. This time the bowl contained blood. She emptied the bowl and rinsed it out. Jim vomited a third time. This time it was more serious and he was bringing up blood clots.

Pam was very worried and again suggested calling a doctor. Jim said he felt strange, "bizarre" was the word he used, but he no longer felt sick and did not want a doctor. He told Pam to go back to bed and said he was going to finish his bath and would join her later. Pam says she felt reassured that Jim was feeling better because his colour had returned a bit. She went back to bed and fell asleep immediately.

She awoke later with a start with no idea how long she had been sleeping. She saw that Jim still hadn't returned to bed and

THE
END

THE END

ran to the bathroom where she found Jim unconscious in the bath. A little blood had trickled from his nose. She tried to shake him awake but it was no use. Then she attempted to get him out of the bath but he was too heavily built for her to move him. In a state of panic and near hysteria, she ran to the phone and called Alan Ronay.

In Ronay's statement to the police he said he thought that Pam telephoned around 8:30am. He said she was crying on the phone and asked him to come over straight away because Jim was unconscious in the bath. He and his girlfriend, the film maker Agnes Varda (Demy), went to the Morrison apartment as fast as they could through the morning rush hour. The Fire Brigade received an emergency call at 9:21am and reached the flat by 9:24am (the station was nearby). This suggests that Ronay did not call them until he reached the flat and saw what was going on, or else Pam telephoned Ronay at 9.20am rather than 8.30am. In one police statement he said that firemen were already present when he arrived. In another he said he telephoned them after seeing Jim in the bath.

When the firemen arrived, a distraught Pam took them straight to the bathroom. The firemen pulled Jim from the bath and put him on the bedroom floor to massage his heart. It was too late. By the time Alan Ronay and Agnes Varda arrived the Fire Brigade were already on the scene but they refused to answer their questions as they went in. Pam was tremendously relieved to see them since she was unable to talk to the firemen as she couldn't speak French. Now Ronay was able to step in as translator. She told them Jim was dead. Ronay didn't want to see the body which by this time was already on the bed, though this contradicts the verbal statement he made to the police.

It's now 9:25am. It was at this time that the police arrived, accompanied by a curious neighbour, Monsieur Chastagnol, who lived on the floor below. Chastagnol walked in and saw what was taking place. His memory is of seeing a body on the floor next to a bed. The body was dressed in normal house clothes and did not appear to be wet. Chastagnol says he was told that Mr. Morrison had just died, possibly from a drugs overdose. Not wishing to intrude further, he returned to his own flat.

The police began their investigation by looking around the

THE
END

flat and at the body. They questioned Pam, Alan, and Agnes Varda. In their examination of the body, they noted it was still supple, the eyes were half open and a little blood was seeping from the right nostril. Jim's left nostril was blocked by a blood clot. His body was naked and after the examination, they covered it with a bedspread.

The Fire Brigade left at 9:47am but the police remained and continued their interviews, then asked Pamela and Ronay to come down to the station later to make formal statements. At 2:30pm the police registered Jim's death at the Town Hall and a death certificate and burial permit were issued. At 3:40pm Pam and Alan went to the police station to make their statements. While they were at the police station, Agnes Varda remained in the apartment to let in Doctor Max Vassille who arrived at 6.00pm. He examined the body and made out his report. Pam, Alan and Agnes spent the evening together, with Pam presumably spending the night at Agnes Varda's apartment where Ronay was staying. Jim's body remained on the bed in the otherwise empty apartment in the rue Beautreillis.

On Sunday, July 4, the police made out their report and it is likely that Pamela and Alan were present at the flat in case the police needed more information. With Jim's body still occupying the bedroom, it must have been a very quiet and sombre day.

By Monday, July 5, rumours were circulating in the press that Jim Morrison was dead. The rumours quickly spread to America and The Doors acting manager Bill Siddons who wasn't immediately alarmed since rumours of Jim's death had been floated before. He made a number of calls to Paris, but both the police and the American Embassy claimed to have no knowledge of an American by that name and description as having died over the week-end. He finally telephoned Pam to find out what was going on. The story goes that she told Bill to come over straight away. He caught the next flight to Paris.

By this time the funeral directors had delivered the coffin and prepared the body, dressing Jim in a suit for burial. On Tuesday, July 6, Pamela, presumably accompanied by Alan Ronay, went to Père Lachaise and purchased a double grave, all they could make available at such short notice. For some reason she told the cemetery office there she was Jim

69

THE END

Morrison's cousin, something the lawyers for her estate corrected six years later. Also that day, Bill Siddons arrived from Los Angeles and went straight to see Pam who told him that Jim was dead. Jet-lagged, worried, mourning the death of his friend, he viewed the coffin and was shown the death certificate. Bill never saw nor asked to see the body.

On Wednesday, July 7, at 9:00am, a hearse with four pallbearers collected the coffin and took it to Père Lachaise for burial. The coffin was lowered into the ground and a few words said over the grave. No clergyman was present. Jim was laid to rest. The only mourners were Pam, Bill Siddons, Alan Ronay, Agnes Varda and another friend, Robin Wertle. Jim's direct family was not represented, the other members of the The Doors were not present, and nor were there any fans to intrude upon their private grief.

Whether Jim's family had been informed of his death at this point we don't know, but it seems unlikely since communication between them and Jim - and by extension Jim's friends and associates - had been minimal for some considerable time by 1971.

The next day, Thursday, July 8, Bill and Pam spent going through Jim's belongings and packing ready for their return to the U.S.A. It was not until their arrival in Los Angeles, on Friday, July 9, that the news was officially released to the press. In a press release, dated the previous day, presumably when it was written, they told the world that Jim Morrison was dead - and already buried. The reason given for the delay in making the announcement was... "Because those who knew him intimately and loved him as a person wanted to escape the notoriety and the circus atmosphere which surrounded the deaths of Janis Joplin and Jimi Hendrix."

That was the story, but I still didn't buy it - at least not every aspect of it. For me there were still too many inconsistencies in the reports of witnesses, so I continued my research.

At the end of March I sent a second letter to Monsieur Chastagnol. I had to be sure that his account of what he saw back on the July 3, 1971, wasn't some kind of error. He told me that he saw Jim Morrison dead, lying on the floor fully dressed, at the foot of his bed, and had been told that the deceased had possibly died of a drug overdose. This information had not

THE END

been mentioned in any of the official statements that I had acquired. His statement contradicted the police version of the incident. Were the police lying? What would be their motive for doing such a thing? The Fire Brigade's account matched that of the police. Could all the people concerned possibly have conspired together to cover up the truth? If so, for what reason?

Maybe the authorities did suspect drugs but felt that it would attract unsavoury publicity and focus attention on the fact that heroin was available in Paris and was not just an American problem. Since both Pamela and Alan were foreign nationals and Pamela, at least, was leaving the country, they may have felt it was prudent to let well alone. If Morrison had used heroin, they did not want to advertise the fact and encourage young French people to try it. If that was how he died, he had paid a high enough price for breaking French law. Was Jim Morrison the "sacrificial lamb"? All this was pure speculation but I felt it was not far from the truth. I had to be sure that Monsieur Chastagnol was not confusing Jim's death with some other tenant, unlikely as this might have been. I wrote a new set of questions and sent the letter off hoping for more surprises.

Monsieur Chastagnol replied on April 3 and stuck absolutely to his version of events:

> "The police did not ask me to go upstairs with them. I just happened to be going upstairs at the same time as them. I followed them up and went into the flat behind them without saying anything. There must have been three of them. I only stayed about two minutes. The body was spread out full length on the floor, at the foot of the bed, was not wet and was wearing house clothes - not that I paid much attention to that particular fact - it was all very quick.
>
> "What time could it have been? Probably about 9 or 9:30 in the morning. It does not mean that he did not die in his bath. I do not know about this; but if that was the case, it would mean that the body would have been dried and dressed before the arrival of the police."

He was convincing enough. Here was Jim dressed and lying

THE END

on the floor, whereas the police report had him naked, covered with a bedspread. It was a big enough difference to merit further investigation. I was also unconvinced by the doctor's explanation as to the cause of death.

Fortunately the pathologist Prof. Austin Gresham resides in Cambridge as professor of Morbid Anatomy of the John Bonnett Clinical Laboratories of Addenbrooke's Hospital. Gresham is regarded as the best in his field in the country and is often sought after to solve unexplained deaths. I telephoned him and explained my problem. He asked me to put it in writing, so on April 24, I mailed him all the details I had on Morrison's death, including photocopies of the police reports and their translations.

His reply was brief and succinct:

> *"Dear Mr. Seymore,*
> *It is likely that the blood from the mouth and nose of Morrison came from an ulcer in the stomach. This and sudden death due both to catecholamine release is a feature of cocaine addiction (particularly Crack).*
> *"Yours sincerely,*
> *G.A. Gresham."*

This was unexpected to say the least. I read the letter again.
So Jim had a stomach ulcer. This accounted for a lot. It certainly figured. Jim had neglected his health abysmally over the years and had been a heavy drinker since his mid teens. The stress of the Miami trials, even the possibility of a prison sentence, could have triggered an ulcer, if he didn't have one already. Was this the explanation? On the morning of his death, did he take a line or two of cocaine which, because of his poor health and a haemorrhaging stomach ulcer, caused his body to go into shock?

Prof. Gresham used the term 'catecholamine release'. Catecholamines are naturally occurring chemicals which are produced by the adrenal glands located just above the kidneys and are similar to adrenalin. In a case of severe blood loss resulting in low blood pressure, catecholamines serve as balancing or stabilizing agents to allow the vital organs to continue functioning. However, if a person lives a life of

physical neglect, as Jim Morrison most certainly did, the
catecholamines will be useless and without prompt medical
assistance the individual will die. This is a generalization but
that's how they work. The cocaine, as I understand it,
rendered the catecholamines powerless and finished him off.

It is apparently very difficult to determine the exact time an
individual dies since room temperature, the position of the
body and many other variables affect the outset of rigor mortis.
It is not an exact science, just informed professional guess
work. To quote Black's Medical Dictionary, by William A.R.
Thomson, 34th Edition:

> *"Four points are important in determining the time
> that has elapsed since death.*
>
> *"Hypostasis, or congestion, begins to appear as livid
> spots on the back, often mistaken for bruises, three hours
> or more after death. It is due to the blood running into
> the vessels in the lowest parts.*
>
> *"Loss of heat begins at once after death, and the body
> has become as cold as the surrounding air after 12 hours,
> though this is delayed by hot weather, death from
> asphyxia, and some other causes.*
>
> *"Rigidity, or rigor-mortis, begins in six hours and takes
> another six to become fully established, remains for
> twelve hours and passes off during the succeeding twelve
> hours. It comes on quickly when extreme exertion has
> been indulged in immediately before death. Conversely, it
> is slow in onset and slight in death from wasting diseases.
> It is slight or absent in children. It begins in the small
> muscles of the eyelids and jaw and then spreads over the
> body.*
>
> *"Putrefaction is variable in time of onset, but usually
> begins in two or three days, as a greenish tint over the
> abdomen."*

There you are, now you know how difficult it is to say at what
time Jim died that morning. It seems to me most likely that he
died between 7:00am and 8:30am and not 5:00am as the official
story has it. In the days preceding Jim's death, he had
complained of breathlessness and difficulty in breathing. It is

THE
END

73

THE END

very likely that he was suffering from anaemia, the condition where there is a lack of red blood cells in the bloodstream and occurs where there has been loss of blood or an inadequate intake of iron from poor diet. Bleeding from the gastro-intestinal tract such as a duodenal or gastric ulcer, if allowed to bleed over a long period of time, will lead to anaemia. The breathing becomes rapid and distressed and the blood-pressure is low. Remember Jim had trouble carrying an armful of logs. It sounds as if Jim was a walking time-bomb, just waiting for the right combination of factors to kill him.

I eventually got round to sending another letter to Lieutenant Colonel Galeraud of the Paris Fire Brigade along with a photo-copy of Monsieur Chastagnol's letter and the Fire Brigade statement made by the police asking for his views on the contradictions between the two reports. He never replied. I wasn't surprised.

I was still intrigued by the fact that there appeared to be two passports floating around that belonged to Jim. Towards the latter part of April I finally telephoned the American Embassy in Paris and spoke Mr. Christopher English, reminding him that I had been in touch with him a year earlier. He remembered. I asked whether their files had any information on Jim's application for a replacement passport after he had supposedly lost it during a trip to Corsica. Mr. English said he would check this out for me and asked me to phone him back. When I called back he had made the search but discovered that their files only go back ten years. Previous to that the files would be with the Department of State in Washington D.C.

I asked him what would have been the procedure in applying for a new passport? He said the old passport and number would have been cancelled, making it invalid and that the new passport would have a new issue and expiry date. The holder would have been instructed not to use the old passport should it turn up. I thanked him for his help and he wished me luck.

But the old passport did turn up and was shown to the police by Pamela in order to identify the body. What happened to the new passport? I called the Department of State in Washington D.C. to see if I would be able to find the details about Jim's passport under the 'Freedom of Information Act'. The lady there said I could have what I needed but - and it was a big "but" - it would take 18 months before I could receive a reply. Well, I don't have 18 months, so I gave that one up. Maybe one day I'll follow it up. I was hoping that maybe Danny Sugerman would help me answer this question as he had seen documents under the Freedom of Information Act so I sent him a fax. He never replied. Thanks Danny.

The business of Morrison's passport was constantly on my mind. Police records showed that his body was identified from the picture on his old passport which was due to expire a month after his death and the whereabouts of his new passport was not mentioned or shown to exist. Maybe he didn't get a new passport, but how could this be checked? Washington certainly wasn't going to assist in a hurry... there had to be another, quicker, way. Of course... Jim would have had to go to a photographer to get his picture taken because the photo had to be a specific size and booth photos would not be accepted. It was therefore a safe bet that somewhere in the 4th district of Paris, in a photographer's darkroom, there existed black and white negatives of Morrison. And, likely as not, the photographer concerned didn't even know who he was or what he had hidden in his storeroom.

I asked Nadine to make further contact with her friend in Paris and ask her to compile a list of photographer's shops in the 4th district. A few days later a list of every photographic shop in Paris arrived in the mail - actually a few pages torn from the French Yellow Pages, and though we tried to call some of the photographers it seemed too thin a line of inquiry to pursue by phone or even in person. Maybe some day someone will come across Jim's passport photo in the belongings of a commercial photographer in the 4th district of Paris. I'm sure it's there somewhere even though it is a needle in a haystack situation.

In the meantime I had also started making inquiries as to the whereabouts of Agnes Varda. The British Film Institute in London confirmed that she still worked in the French film industry and her agents, Cinetamaris in the 14th district of Paris, informed me that she was working on location in the French countryside. I wrote to Ms Varda care of the agency but it was in vain as my letter, which contained many questions, went unanswered despite several reminders.

THE END

75

One other peculiar lead turned up during the later stages of my inquiries, one that implied Marianne Faithfull had somehow been involved during the 24 hours that Jim died. This rumour had been floated for years and largely forgotten, but it resurfaced again with the publication of John Densmore's book *Riders On The Storm* in the autumn of 1990.

Densmore tells of how he was once interviewed by a Los Angeles disc jockey who inquired about Marianne's role in the death of Morrison, but Densmore had no knowledge of her involvement at all. Curiously, though, Densmore was the only member of The Doors with whom Jim spoke - by phone - from Paris during his final days.

In the summer of 1971, it states in Densmore's book, Marianne was living in Paris with a French Count with whom Pamela had once had a brief relationship during an earlier visit to Paris. Like Pam, both Marianne and the Count were regular heroin users.

This version of the story alleges that when Pam awoke on the morning of Jim's death she found the bathroom door locked with Jim - presumably - inside. Since she was unable to force open the door her second instinct was to call her friend the Count, who arrived twenty minutes later with Marianne in tow. Together the three of them forced open the bathroom door to find Jim dead in the tub inside.

At this point the Count and Marianne, not wishing to become mixed up in the death of a famous rock star and fearing the attendant headlines that would follow, made their excuses and left. A further reason for their hasty departure was the unwelcome likelihood of their being separated from their drug stash for an unacceptable period of time while undergoing lengthy interrogation by police. They left, requesting Pam not to mention their arrival and departure to anyone else, ever, and Pam kept her word unto death.

After Marianne and the Count departed Pam phoned Alan Ronay and Agnes Varda, and implied to them that they were the first to hear the news. '

According to Densmore's book, when Bill Siddons arrived at the apartment he opened a carved wooden box which he found on a coffee table and discovered it contained heroin. He came to the conclusion that Jim must have taken some of this heroin, believing it to have been cocaine, and overdosed as a result. In which case Pam would have been riddled with guilt because Jim had found her stash and snorted it under the assumption that it was cocaine. All of which begs another question: wasn't the apartment searched thoroughly by the police when they were called after the discovery of Jim body? If Bill Siddons could find the heroin so easily, then a team of police surely ought to have found it.

Marianne Faithfull's agent, Peter Charles of the Asgard Agency in London, contacted Marianne on my behalf in a bid to confirm or deny the allegations in Densmore's book. "Yes... Marianne was in Paris at the time with her then boyfriend but she never met Jim Morrison in her life," he told me. "She wishes she had, though."

But did she 'meet' him after he'd died?

"We have always been aware of the various rumours about this and other stories and there is no truth in this one either," he said.

In the end I sent Peter Charles a copy of the page from John Densmore's book which related to this story. His only comment was: "If we believed everything we read in books, then the world would be flat."

While trying to interest a publisher in my findings, I unexpectedly came upon Jonathan Dolger's telephone number in New York. This was a break as I very much wanted to speak with this man. You remember he was the guy who received Jim's telegram the day before he died. I phoned him and made the usual introduction.

"Oh my God," he said. It was as though he had been woken up from an old nightmare.

I asked him about the telegram but he said that he no longer had it. At first he thought maybe his former employers had it in their files, his memory of that time was vague after so many years but he did recall that Jim sent him a cable because he wanted to change the cover of his poetry book *The Lords* and *The New Creatures*. He agreed with me that it could have been anyone that sent the telegram. Then he recalled that a man whose name he had forgotten contacted him to ask if he could have the telegram that Jim sent. This was a month after Jim died and the person said he was with Jim when he died.

THE
END

THE
END

I asked if the name was Alan Ronay? Dolger said the name was familiar but he couldn't be sure, however he did remember what the man looked like. I thanked Jonathan for his help and apologized for coming out of the blue. He didn't mind at all. He said, in a quiet sombre tone, "I liked Jim very much. He was a very nice man." I put the phone down. This call had an effect on me. I felt that I had intruded on someone's private grief even though nearly twenty years had passed. Why would Alan Ronay want the telegram? A rock souvenir? Was there something in the telegram that he didn't think should get out? I doubt if we will ever know the answer to that one.

Why hasn't someone tried to investigate Morrison's death before? The lack of official proof has allowed rumours, lies, suspicion, and the myth of some kind of cover-up conspiracy to fester over the years. To get through all the red tape wasn't easy. I am more than certain Alan Ronay, Agnes Varda, Bill Siddons and a few other close friends know more than they have revealed in public. It is quite likely that the surviving members of The Doors also know more than they have made public.

Maybe the whole myth about Jim Morrison still being alive was created deliberately in order to sustain interest in The Doors and their music. It's an attractive myth and record companies have done far worse things to promote sales over the years. If someone asked me whether I thought Jim Morrison was still alive, I would say the odds in favour are only about 1%. That is because Pamela and the emergency services were the only people to see a body and its identification was made by Pam and with reference to an old passport. The police accepted this and had no reason not to. They took Pam at her word that it was Jim Morrison.

I cannot see Pam and Jim going to great lengths to get a real corpse, though it is just about possible that a friend of theirs died in the apartment and they realized that this was just the opportunity to disappear for which Jim had been waiting. But this is just a fantasy - after all, if Jim wanted to get away from it all he could simply have retired and remained in France where he was not all that well known. That way he would not have had to break up with Pamela.

Pamela's subsequent life also belies the idea that Jim was

alive in hiding. She rapidly degenerated into heroin addiction, made a number of suicide attempts, including one occasion when she drove a truck straight into the clothes shop, Themis, that Jim bought for her before they went to France. On April 25, 1974, three years after Jim's death, she died in her Hollywood apartment of a heroin overdose, apparently unable to get over Jim's death, and unable to start a fresh life for herself. There was certainly no evidence that she sneaked away to visit him in hiding and it is unlikely that she would have colluded in a move which would have resulted in the break up of their relationship. In many ways, her subsequent life as a grieving widow is the greatest proof we have that Jim is dead.

So is there still a mystery, or was it just a case of bureaucratic blunders by the Paris police and the American embassy, both of which initially denied any knowledge of Morrison's death? To me there is still plenty of reason to question the actual cause of death, if not the death itself. At the time Morrison was in Paris, many people on the French rock scene thought that heroin was a tremendously hip thing to use. To the drug pushers of the rue de Seine, the idea that Morrison did not use heroin would have been almost inconceivable, particularly since Pamela used it and therefore bought it from someone. In 1971 rock was still regarded as a revolutionary, anti-establishment force, particularly in France where hard rock music constituted only a very small percentage of the total of all records sold. To know anything about American and British underground music in France in those days was a "life-style" statement all of its own.

Morrison often visited the Rock'n'Roll Circus in the rue de Seine, the main Parisian hangout for the music business crowd, and it is certain that the drug dealers there would have fallen over each other for the honour and status of giving - or, better still, selling - him some of their wares. Since he did not speak French, it is easy to imagine him accepting some heroin, thinking it was cocaine. Then again, Morrison was a great experimenter. Maybe he decided to try it, not realizing that it was many times more powerful than the street heroin in the States.

Whatever happened, it was a squalid end for such a talent. A squalid end, in a squalid grave. I'm surprised that the Morrison family have not had their son's remains returned to

THE END

the States where they can oversee the condition of his grave, or that the surviving Doors have not put up the money to have the grave at Père Lachaise tidied up and maintained in a dignified manner. It is still a shrine to the group - their group - but a very grubby one.

My reason for undertaking this research in the first place, apart from wanting to become the photographer who took a shot of Jim 19 years after he 'died', was because even after all these years I still receive strength and energy from listening to the lyrics and music of The Doors.

Where ever he may be, Jim Morrison lives on - in his music. R.I.P. Jim Morrison.